Confronting the German Idealist Tradition

The philosophical activity of modern Germany represents a peak in the history of philosophy beginning from Thales in ancient Greece. This book attempts to reconsider the conventional image of 19th-century German philosophy. To this end, it illuminates a forgotten philosophical stream contemporaneous with so-called "German idealism."

From this perspective, this book examines the philosophy of Jakob Friedrich Fries, a philosopher contemporaneous and in confrontation with Hegel. By examining Fries' standpoint, the book attempts to reconstruct the picture of 19th-century German philosophy. In the 19th and 20th centuries, philosophers other than Kant, Fichte, Schelling, and Hegel – especially Fries – had a significant influence on the history of philosophy, constituting an alternative genealogy to Hegel's. One might say that the conventional history of philosophy conceals Fries' influence. Accordingly, this book will examine Fries' philosophy, the Friesian school established by E.F. Apelt, and the Neo-Friesian school formed by Leonard Nelson.

This approach reveals the factiousness of the history of philosophy that starts from Kant, passes through German idealism and flows into the Neo-Kantian movement. It will provide a new viewpoint from which to reconsider the history of German philosophy.

Tadahiro Oota is an Assistant Professor at the National Institute of Technology, Numazu College (Japan). He is the author of a paper titled "Jakob Friedrich Fries as an Opponent of German Idealism," in: *Anti-Idealism: Re-interpreting a German Discourse*, De Gruyter, 2019.

Confronting the German Idealist Tradition
Jakob Friedrich Fries, the Friesian School and the Neo-Friesian School

Tadahiro Oota

LONDON AND NEW YORK

First published 2023
by Routledge
4 Park Square, Milton Park, Abingdon, Oxon OX14 4RN

and by Routledge
605 Third Avenue, New York, NY 10158

Routledge is an imprint of the Taylor & Francis Group, an informa business

© 2023 Tadahiro Oota

The right of Tadahiro Oota to be identified as author of this work has been asserted in accordance with sections 77 and 78 of the Copyright, Designs and Patents Act 1988.

All rights reserved. No part of this book may be reprinted or reproduced or utilised in any form or by any electronic, mechanical, or other means, now known or hereafter invented, including photocopying and recording, or in any information storage or retrieval system, without permission in writing from the publishers.

Trademark notice: Product or corporate names may be trademarks or registered trademarks, and are used only for identification and explanation without intent to infringe.

British Library Cataloguing-in-Publication Data
A catalogue record for this book is available from the British Library

Library of Congress Cataloging-in-Publication Data
Names: Ōta, Tadahiro, 1990-author.
Title: Confronting the German idealist tradition: Jakob Friedrich Fries, the Friesian school and the neo-Friesian school/Tadahiro Oota.
Description: Abingdon, Oxon; New York, NY: Routledge, 2023. | Includes bibliographical references.
Identifiers: LCCN 2023008396 (print) | LCCN 2023008397 (ebook) | ISBN 9781032522982 (hardback) | ISBN 9781032523019 (paperback) | ISBN 9781003406006 (ebook)
Subjects: LCSH: Fries, Jakob Friedrich, 1773-1843. | Idealism, German. | Philosophy, German–19th century.
Classification: LCC B2978 .O83 2023 (print) | LCC B2978 (ebook) | DDC 193–dc23/eng/20230322
LC record available at https://lccn.loc.gov/2023008396
LC ebook record available at https://lccn.loc.gov/2023008397

ISBN: 9781032522982 (hbk)
ISBN: 9781032523019 (pbk)
ISBN: 9781003406006 (ebk)

DOI: 10.4324/9781003406006

Typeset in Times New Roman
by Deanta Global Publishing Services, Chennai, India

dedicated to my parents

Contents

Preface ix

1 **Introduction** 1
  1.1 Why should 19th-century German philosophy be addressed today? 1
    1.1.1 What is the history of philosophy? 1
    1.1.2 Nineteenth-century German philosophy 2
    1.1.3 The dominant schematization of 19th-century German philosophy 3
    1.1.4 The problem of 19th-century Germany 4
  1.2 Why should we begin with the reconstruction of Fries' philosophy? 5
    1.2.1 A problem of 19th-century Germany reconsidered 5
    1.2.2 Receptions of Fries' philosophy in the history of philosophy 6
    1.2.3 Problems with the reception of Fries for research in the history of philosophy 10
  Notes 14

2 **Jakob Friedrich Fries' philosophy** 16
  2.1 Fries' conception of a critique of reason 16
    2.1.1 Fries' methodological standpoint in philosophy 16
    2.1.2 Formation of the method of philosophy: Confronting Fichte and Schelling 35

2.2 On the construction of a metaphysical system: From the viewpoint of the method of philosophy 40
   2.2.1 Feeling of truth 41
   2.2.2 The thing in itself in Fries' philosophy 47
Notes 51

3 The Friesian and Neo-Friesian schools   58

3.1 The Friesian school 58
   3.1.1 The rise of the Friesian school 59
   3.1.2 Ernst Friedrich Apelt's views 60
   3.1.3 Matthias Jacob Schleiden's methodological perspective 66
   3.1.4 Conclusion 71
3.2 The Neo-Friesian school 71
   3.2.1 Nelson and the rise of the Neo-Friesian school 71
   3.2.2 Nelson's reception of Fries' philosophy 72
   3.2.3 The Neo-Friesian school's battle against Neo-Kantianism 76
   3.2.4 The Neo-Friesian school and the analytic tradition 82
Notes 89

4 Conclusion   93

Bibliography   97
Index   103

Preface

Tadahiro Oota

This book is a translation of *Another History of 19th-Century German Philosophy*, first published in 2022 in Japanese. It began as a doctoral thesis submitted to Kyoto University in 2020.

The book attempts to reassess the conventional image of 19th-century German philosophy. It deals specifically with the work of Jakob Friedrich Fries, a philosophical rival of Hegel. By examining Fries' standpoint, this book attempts to reconstruct the picture of 19th-century German philosophy. In the 19th and 20th centuries, thinkers such as Fries had a significant influence on the history of philosophy, constituting an alternative genealogy to Hegel's, beyond that of Kant, Fichte, and Schelling. One might argue that conventional histories conceal the influence of Fries' philosophy. This book will examine Fries' philosophy, the Friesian school established by E.F. Apelt, and the Neo-Friesian school formed by Leonard Nelson. Its approach reveals the factionalism of the history of philosophy that begins with Kant, passes through German idealism, and flows into the Neo-Kantian movement. The book will provide a new viewpoint from which to reconsider the history of German philosophy.

I would like to sincerely express my gratitude to Professor Emeritus Dr. Shigeru Fukutani, who was my supervisor during undergraduate, master's, and doctoral studies, and always inspired me to approach the history of philosophy through emphasis on "cross-sections," as propounded in his book *Saggi sulla filosofia kantiana* (in Japanese). I would also like to thank Professor Dr. Taiju Okochi, who was my supervisor during the final year of my doctorate and who prompted my interest in reconsidering the schematization of 19th-century German philosophy through his paper "What is 'German idealism'?: Or, why 'German idealism' should not be so-called?" (in Japanese). I am also grateful to Professor Dr. Yasuo Deguchi, Professor Dr. Masashi Nakahata, and Professor Dr. Jun Otsuka, who also supervised my doctoral thesis and whose comments on my work were invaluable.

I also extend my thanks to two anonymous reviewers, whose constructive recommendations and suggestions helped to improve the book significantly. Note that [ ] in the text means supplement by the quoter, and [...] means omission by the quoter.

Tadahiro Oota
Shizuoka, Japan
1 February 2023

1 Introduction

1.1 Why should 19th-century German philosophy be addressed today?

1.1.1 What is the history of philosophy?

One of the episodes of highest achievement in the history of philosophy, ever since Thales in ancient Greece, may be found in the philosophical activity of modern Germany. Modern German philosophy is defined by the philosophical period in which Kant and Hegel were dominant, Kant belonging to the 18th century and Hegel to the 19th. The public image of 19th-century philosophy consists of so-called German idealism: A philosophical tradition symbolized by Fichte, Schelling, and Hegel. This concept of German idealism surely implies a one-sided interpretation of 19th-century German philosophy. Although the dominant image thereof is still one characterized by the concept of German idealism, this book aims to re-illuminate another stream of thought in 19th-century German philosophy, and one that remains ignored. To do so, this book investigates Jakob Friedrich Fries and the philosophy of the Friesian and Neo-Friesian schools.

What kind of relationship do philosophy and its history have? Insomuch as philosophy is a subject that retains the name φιλοσοφία from ancient Greek, it cannot be defined only by its topics or by its method of approaching its object of inquiry. Rather, as in Whitehead's remark that philosophy characterizes the European philosophical tradition as a series of footnotes on Plato,[1] philosophical thought has developed through its reception of, and confrontation with, philosophy since the ancient Greeks. In this sense, philosophy has long had a relationship with the history of philosophy, whether a positive or a negative one. From this viewpoint, the history of philosophy is not a mere chronological series of past philosophers, but rather philosophy gains its meaning only through the history of philosophy. Philosophy, therefore, is a part of each episode of intellectual activity, one that raises questions in accordance with the constraints and context of its period,

DOI: 10.4324/9781003406006-1

confronting the philosophical problems that arose among the ancient Greeks. The history of philosophy can be characterized as the chronological self-awareness of philosophy in respect to the succession of these episodes. That is, philosophical investigation can never be formulated separately from the constraints and context of the time when it developed. In this respect, as Shigeru Fukutani notes, philosophy can be construed as a cross section of the history of philosophy.[2] The texts of past philosophers are therefore open to diverse interpretation in accordance with their interpreters in different periods and contexts. This applies also to the history of the reception of philosophy, and to any description of the history of philosophy.

Kuno Fischer, a historian of philosophy in 19th-century Germany, and one of the historians who created a contemporary schematization of the history of philosophy, said that philosophy cannot be measured by the rightness of its conclusions or evaluated as a collection of those conclusions. Rather, philosophy should be understood in terms of the problems it addresses.

> In respect of the truth in philosophy, or, in respect of the multiplicity of historical systems of it, I would like to repeat this sentence for the audience: "The true problem is also the truth."
>
> (Fischer [1862], p. 20)

Fischer located the purpose of philosophy in neither a series of arguments nor the aggregation of conclusions, but rather in the problem of philosophy that underlies the history of philosophy. Confronting this can bring forth a new perspective to illuminate our own historical – and philosophical – standpoint. This is what Fischer, a great historian of philosophy, finally achieved.

1.1.2 Nineteenth-century German philosophy

Such an understanding of the history of philosophy arose for the first time in 19th-century German philosophy. In this sense, 19th-century German philosophy is a stream of thought which leads us directly to these ideas about the history of philosophy. This was the period in which Fichte, Hegel, and Schelling's work developed from the fruits of Immanuel Kant's critical philosophy. The same period produced such famous philosophers as Nietzsche and Kierkegaard, so 19th-century German philosophy gives us a public image of philosophy in general. Further characteristics of 19th-century German philosophy can be found in its continuity with modern thought. Concepts such as society, freedom, and causality were understood and thematized in a modern way as a result of 19th-century Germans' conceptualization of many ideas constructing our daily life or contemporary science.

How, then, has 19th-century Germany been schematized until today? Under the concept of German idealism: The vulgar figure of the history of philosophy from Kant to Hegel, or Kant–Fichte–Schelling–Hegel. When was this schematization produced? In fact, it was in 19th-century Germany that the history of philosophy as a discipline developed. Before the 19th century, only a few historians of philosophy existed, such as Johann Jakob Brucker, whose history of philosophy was merely an enumeration of past philosophers. Conceptions of the history of philosophy as an intellectual chronology, consisting of a reception of, and confrontation with, each previous period, first appeared in 19th-century Germany: For example, Wilhelm Gottlieb Tennemann's *Geschichte der Philosophie*, Neo-Hegelians' and Neo-Kantians' histories of philosophy, and others. In particular, many eminent philosophers have made use of the history of philosophy produced by the Neo-Kantians, including eastern philosophers like Kitaro Nishida (1870–1945).

1.1.3 The dominant schematization of 19th-century German philosophy

The history of 19th-century philosophy itself, however, faces further problems. The schematization of the history of 19th-century German philosophy was itself established in 19th-century Germany. Therefore, 19th-century Germany both (i) produced its own contemporaneous philosophy and (ii) defined the history of philosophy by placing itself at the forefront of that history. Nineteenth-century German philosophy here differs from both previous eras and the rest of the modern period, in which this 19th-century schematization of the history of philosophy was already presupposed. Therefore, 19th-century German philosophy was itself a kind of self-promotion of 19th-century German philosophers, especially the Neo-Hegelians and Neo-Kantians who won the hegemonic entitlement to describe the history of philosophy. This situation has left us a distorted history of 19th-century German philosophy, a one-sidedness in the modern schematization of philosophy which prevents our grasping the history of philosophy, especially that of the late 19th and early 20th centuries.

The vulgar image of 19th-century German philosophy can be summarized as follows: After Kant's death, Fichte developed his philosophy, based on "I"; Schelling developed his standpoint, based on nature; and Hegel summarized both Fichte and Schelling and developed his own standpoint, based on absolute spirit. These philosophers constitute a linear structure called German idealism, and Hegel reigns at the top of the structure.

This constitutes the understanding of the history of philosophy that persists today. For example, Hirschberger's work, often described as a canonical account of the history of philosophy, presupposes such a schematization.

4 Introduction

Of course, such a schematization seems outmoded from the perspective of more recent research on the history of philosophy. As is well known, Schelling developed a new standpoint, termed positive philosophy, after Hegel's death; and many philosophers other than German idealists – such as Reinhold, Jacobi, Hölderlin, Niethammer, and Fries – were active in this period. From this viewpoint, the linear structure of Kant–Fichte–Schelling–Hegel is too arbitrary a schematization, requiring deconstruction and reconsideration. In recent studies of German philosophy, the term "classical German philosophy" is preferred to "German idealism."

1.1.4 The problem of 19th-century Germany

The linear schematization of German idealism remains dominant today, despite its reconsideration in recent studies, especially in the 21st century. This schematization of philosophy has had a significant influence on the history of philosophy as has been understood. For example, Habermas' monumental work, *Auch eine Geschichte der Philosophie*, attempts to reconstruct the history of philosophy, declaring itself to be another history of philosophy led by arguments about knowing and believing. His book, however, also follows the framing of German idealism without reconsidering its validity.

In addition, recent critical investigation of German idealism remains bound to the linear structure of Kant–Fichte–Schelling–Hegel as a line of dominant philosophers which recent studies of German philosophy also presuppose, simply attempting to illuminate its precise aspect. Even these recent studies have understood philosophers other than Kant, Fichte, Schelling, and Hegel to be less important philosophers, and the Kant–Fichte–Schelling–Hegel line remains dominant.

In this situation, this book reconsiders the conventional image of 19th-century German philosophy. It investigates the philosophy of Jakob Friedrich Fries, a philosopher contemporaneous and in confrontation with Hegel. Based on Fries' standpoint, this book reconstructs the picture of 19th-century German philosophy. In the 19th and 20th centuries, philosophers other than Kant, Fichte, Schelling, and Hegel constituted a separate genealogy from the Hegelian one, and they, especially Fries, had a significant influence on the history of philosophy. The conventional history of philosophy is a history that conceals the influence of Fries' philosophy. This book will examine Fries' philosophy, that of the Friesian school established by Ernst Friedrich Apelt, and the Neo-Friesian school formed by Leonard Nelson. This reveals the factiousness of the history of philosophy that starts with Kant, continues through German idealism, and flows into the Neo-Kantian movement, providing a new viewpoint from which to reconsider German philosophy.[3]

This book owes a great deal to Frederick Beiser's work *The Genesis of Neo-Kantianism: 1796–1880* (Beiser [2014]). Beiser claims that "the origins of neo-Kantianism are shrouded in mystery"[4] and attempts to find its origin in a "lost tradition"[5] consisting of Fries, Herbart, and Beneke. Beiser emphasizes a role for these philosophers which is distinct from German idealism. According to Beiser, Fries, Herbart, and Beneke "had so many attitudes, values and beliefs in common that one is justified in regarding them as a distinct tradition"[6] – one distinguished from the German idealist tradition.

In contrast, according to Beiser, Fries' thought came episodically before the rise of Neo-Kantianism[7] and, in this sense, Fries seems to be regarded as a boundary of the Neo-Kantian tradition. However, Fries' philosophy was opposed not only to the so-called German idealist tradition, but also, in the shape of the Friesian school's activity, to the Neo-Kantian movement. Therefore, the battle between Nelson and Neo-Kantian philosophers should not be regarded merely as an internal conflict within a Neo-Kantian movement, but rather as a confrontation between two philosophical schools. From this viewpoint, this book provides an overview of Fries', the Friesian school's, and the Neo-Friesian school's thought, especially in its epistemological aspects, and as opposed not only to the German idealist tradition, but also to Hegelianism and Neo-Kantianism.

1.2 Why should we begin with the reconstruction of Fries' philosophy?

1.2.1 A problem of 19th-century Germany reconsidered

Why then should we begin with the reconstruction of Fries' philosophy? This chapter examines the historical reception of Fries' philosophy, as well as his overlooked influence on the history of philosophy, in order to clarify the limits of the historical framework known as German idealism.

Nineteenth-century German philosophy has traditionally been understood using a linear structuring scheme: German idealism begins with Kant, develops via Fichte and Schelling, and ends with Hegel. Some researchers have recently criticized this schematization of German philosophy as out of date, and many who take this view are working to unearth and re-evaluate forgotten philosophers of the period in order to reconstruct the history of philosophy as a constellation of philosophers. These researchers employ the term "classical German philosophy" instead of "German idealism" to refer to the constellation of 19th-century German philosophical movements.

Although recent research has re-evaluated 19th-century German philosophers other than the German idealists, this approach presupposes that

6 Introduction

it was the German idealists who had a significant influence on the history of philosophy, and that other philosophers had neither the dominance of the German idealists during their lifetime nor any recognizable influence on the history of philosophy in later periods. Consequently, some 19th-century German philosophers remain ignored, or at least misunderstood, in this re-evaluated history of philosophy, which retains the imprint of the old narrative and thus fails to reveal the true nature of classical German philosophy. This chapter examines the historical reception of Jacob Friedrich Fries (1773–1843), a 19th-century German philosopher contemporaneous with German idealism and best known for his *New Critique of Reason* (*Neue Kritik der Vernunft*[8]).[9] Fries is a typical example of such an overlooked philosopher, and this chapter aims to illuminate his hidden influence.

The chapter first describes the process through which Fries' philosophy came to be regarded as psychologism. It then examines references by his contemporaries to Fries' philosophy, as well as others by a Japanese philosopher, which show that they more accurately understood Fries' philosophy than has previously been believed.

1.2.2 Receptions of Fries' philosophy in the history of philosophy

1.2.2.1 Herbart's assessment: An emphasis on psychology[10]

The first notable philosopher who criticized Fries' philosophy by declaring it to be psychologism was Johann Friedrich Herbart. In his *General Metaphysics and the Beginnings of the Philosophical Doctrine of Nature* (*Allgemeine Metaphysik, nebst den Anfängen der philosophischen Naturlehre*), Herbart identified empirical psychology as the essence of Kant's philosophy, and referred to Fries as a typical example of a philosopher who revealed and expanded the role of empirical psychology therein.

> The larger part of Kant's doctrine (which *Fries* and others have treated) depends on the fabled [*fabelhaft*] psychology; and it is filled with all possible fallacies that can occur from psychology on the one hand, or be caused by analogies on the other.
> (Herbart [1828], p. 121)

Herbart thus criticized Kant's philosophy as a standpoint based on psychology.

> Fries had correctly noticed that there is no evident ground except for empirical psychology that underlies Kantian critique.
> (Herbart [1828], p. 245)

Introduction 7

Herbart's aim here was to reduce the essence of Kant's critique to empirical psychology, to criticize it as a traditional false psychology, and to reconstruct a new empirical psychology, based on Herbart's own metaphysics. Herbart referred to Fries in order to authorize his own interpretation of Kant's critique, in the process overemphasizing the role of psychology in Fries' philosophy and characterizing Fries' standpoint as a psychological approach to Kant's philosophy.

1.2.2.2 Hegelian philosophers' critique: Distancing Fries from Kant's philosophy

Herbart's characterization of Fries' philosophy as psychologism was followed by criticism from Hegelian philosophers, who formulated the schematization of German idealism that remains dominant today, as well as the stereotypical image of Fries' philosophy. Kuno Fischer, a Hegelian and the first great opponent of the Friesian school, thematized and objected to Fries' philosophy in a lecture delivered in 1862.[11] He divided German philosophers in Jena into two schools: That to which Reinhold, Fichte, Schelling, and Hegel belonged, and the other, to which Fries belonged.[12] Fischer called them the oldest and the youngest Kantian school, and regarded the oldest as the proper development of Kantian philosophy.[13]

> According to Fries, the basic science of philosophy is therefore not metaphysics but anthropology as a doctrine of inner nature, i.e., a psychic anthropology. [...] Kant's critique did not aim to be anthropological. Here is a difference between Kant and Fries, as well as the need for Fries to renew the critique of reason in his sense. He made it in his *New Critique of Reason*, which is, however, nothing but an anthropological conversion of Kant's critique of reason, a translation of the critique of reason into the language of empirical psychology to a great extent.
>
> (Fischer [1862], p. 14)

Fischer addressed the following question: "Is the critique of reason anthropological, and can it be so?"[14] He answered negatively, targeting Fries' decisive doctrine that *a priori* cognition can be empirically recognized. Fischer denied this doctrine, and rejected Fries' philosophy as follows:

> Now, if the critique of reason is only psychological and therefore merely empirical, how can the objects of a critique's insight be *a priori*? [...] Fries objects as follows: What the critique of reason investigates is *a priori*, but the investigation itself is *a posteriori*. [...] And just here is

8 Introduction

the πρῶτον ψεῦδος [first mistake] in Friesian philosophy. What is *a priori* can never be recognized *a posteriori*.

(Fischer [1862], p. 18)

This shows how Fischer formulated Fries' critique of reason with the terms "anthropology" and "empirical psychology." His critique of Fries thus represents a typical schematization of Fries' philosophy as one that deviated from Kant by emphasizing the role of empirical psychology.

Johann Eduard Erdmann, another Hegelian philosopher, agreed with Fischer's claim. In his *Outline of the History of Philosophy* (*Grundrisss der Geschichte der Philosophie*), Erdmann summarized Fries' standpoint:

> As his main deviance from *Kant*, *Fries* himself explains that he transformed Kant's investigations into an empirical-psychological or anthropological one. By doing this, Fries distanced himself from the "preoccupation of the transcendental."
>
> (Erdmann [1866], p. 397)

Erdmann emphasized the difference between Fries' standpoint and Kant's philosophy, criticizing it as a defect of Fries' philosophy.

1.2.2.3 Neo-Kantian philosophers' schematization: Performed as psychologism

The Hegelian characterization and critique of Fries' philosophy were followed by those of the Neo-Kantian philosophers, who established the theory of the history of philosophy that produced its still-popular schematization. The first Neo-Kantian philosopher to characterize Fries' philosophy as psychologism was Otto Liebmann.[15] Liebmann accepted Fischer's conclusion,[16] and criticized Fries as follows:

> Among misunderstandings that can be made against the Kantian critique, it is the worst misunderstanding to regard it as a psychological one. Moreover, Fries' misunderstanding is not only this. [...] We can summarize our judgments on this point by Kuno Fischer with a short sentence: *What is* a priori *can never be recognized* a posteriori.
>
> (Liebmann [1865], p. 151)

As such, Liebmann rejected Fries' philosophy by claiming that it was not an improvement on Kant's philosophy, but only a retrogression to Locke. While he followed Fischer's critique of Fries' philosophy and emphasized how Fries' standpoint deviated from Kant's critique, Liebmann simultaneously shifted the key word used to characterize Fries' philosophy from "anthropology" to "psychology." Liebmann's critique of Fries' philosophy was followed by that of another famous Neo-Kantian: Wilhelm Windelband.[17] In his *History of Modern Philosophy* (*Geschichte der neueren Philosophie*), Windelband discussed Fries and Beneke in the section entitled "psychologism":

> The most creative progress of philosophical spirits is evidently included in this metaphysical struggle of Post-Kantian philosophy. Next to all this metaphysical struggle, however, there is a series of attempts of another sort, which try to translate the Kantian principle of the self-cognition of human reason into the language of empirical psychology, and to move the underlying research of cognitive theory into the anthropological experience with full awareness. [...] One of the most important philosophers of this sort is exactly the first philosopher who behaves in this way, i.e., of empirical-psychological justification of the Kantian system itself. In his *New Critique of Reason* (1807), *Jacob Friedrich Fries* [...] has attempted to base Kantian doctrine on a psychological conception, which he has precisely confirmed, both substantially and terminologically, in the *Handbook of Psychic Anthropology* (1820), and further accomplished in his other, innumerable books, which cover all parts of philosophy.
>
> (Windelband [1880], p. 386f.)

This shows how Windelband locates the point of Fries' philosophy in the "way of empirical-psychological justification." This characterization of Fries' standpoint exaggerates the psychologistic aspect of Fries' philosophy. Continuing, Windelband summarized Fries' standpoint as follows:

> In the case of Fries, theories [given from Kantian philosophy] appear as the doctrine of an empirical psychology based on the common ground of a merely anthropological distinction, and this is Fries' particular and independent position [in the history of philosophy].
>
> (Ibid., p. 390)

Thus, the interpretation of Fries' philosophy as a form of psychologism was finalized by Windelband's description of the history of philosophy, renowned as a major resource for knowledge of that history in the modern age. The result was that Fries' philosophy disappeared from the legitimate genealogy of the history of German philosophy in the 19th century.

Fries' philosophy, then, was at first connected with psychology as an authentic interpretation of Kant's philosophy, in order to present the grounds

10 *Introduction*

of Kant's philosophy as a fallacious empirical psychology. Hegelian philosophers later rejected the idea that Fries' philosophy was an authentic interpretation of Kant's philosophy, to which they characterized it as a fallacious psychological and anthropological approach. Neo-Kantian philosophers ultimately labeled Fries' philosophy psychologism, cementing its image as a collateral branch of 19th-century German philosophy that transformed Kant's philosophy into a psychologistic one.

1.2.2.4 Contemporary schematization of Fries' philosophy

In this context, many contemporary interpreters of Fries' philosophy also consider it a psychologistic one. A typical example of such interpretations of Fries' philosophy can be found in Gary Hatfield's schematization of it. For example, Hatfield summarizes Fries' efforts as follows:

> Fries took himself primarily to be correcting Kant's failure to realize that his investigation of the knower was really an empirical investigation through inner sense (and theoretical reflection upon the givens thereof).
>
> (Hatfield [1990], p. 111)

Hatfield, then, regards Fries' philosophical methodology as an investigation "through inner sense," and here Hatfield finds the characteristics of psychologism in Fries' philosophy. Hatfield then naively emphasizes Fries' argument about "Kant's blindness to the psychological foundations of his own position"[18] – although Fries' reference to empirical psychology should be interpreted in a limited context, as the following chapter of this book will discuss. On this point, Hatfield's interpretation of Fries' philosophy can be regarded as a stereotype of its characterization as psychologism.

1.2.3 Problems with the reception of Fries for research in the history of philosophy

1.2.3.1 Fries' Philosophy according to his contemporaries

As shown above, the characterization of Fries' philosophy as psychologism arose through its historical reception by the Hegelian and Neo-Kantian philosophers who established a canonical schematization of the history of philosophy. This chapter illuminates aspects of Fries' contemporaries' reception of his philosophy which have been overlooked.

The facile interpretation of Fries' philosophy as psychologism may influence the reconstruction of other philosophers' thought, distorting the

Introduction   11

history of philosophy itself. Fries' contemporaries did not regard his philosophy as psychologism. A typical example is Arthur Schopenhauer's reading note on Fries' *New Critique of Reason*. While developing his own philosophical standpoint, Schopenhauer read Fries' book and left the following comments:

> It is nonsense to distinguish between seeing [*Sehen*] and knowing [*Wissen*] that one sees, because the latter is included in the former. It is also nonsense to distinguish between knowing mathematical and philosophical laws and knowing of such knowing [*Wissen von diesem Wissen*], because the latter is therefore mere abstract knowledge [*Wissen*], a compendium, a reduction of the former.
>
> (Schopenhauer [1967], p. 361)

This comment corresponds to Fries' description in the *New Critique of Reason*. Seeing and knowing here suggest the recognition of objects through reason. Knowing of knowing, conversely, means reason's self-cognition, i.e., philosophizing or a critique of reason. Schopenhauer did not use such words as "psychology" or "anthropology" to characterize Fries' philosophy, unlike many Hegelian and Post-Kantian philosophers in later periods. While Schopenhauer opposes Fries here, his notebook suggests that (at least one of) Fries' contemporaries had correctly understood the crucial point of his philosophy.

1.2.3.2 Hegel's reading of Fries' philosophy

Ignorance of Fries' philosophy also hinders comprehension of Hegel's philosophical development. In fact, Hegel might have understood Fries' doctrine more accurately than previous researchers have suggested.

When researchers have examined Hegel's critique of Fries, they have often noted his criticism of Fries' political thought in the *Outlines of the Philosophy of Right* (*Grundlinien der Philosophie des Rechts*), in which Hegel refers to Fries' short "Speech on the German Student Union" (*Rede an die deutschen Burschen*).[19] Previous researchers have, therefore, focused on Hegel's conflict with Fries over their political thought, as well as their competition in their careers, and reduced Hegel's criticism to personal animosity.

However, Hegel's manuscript suggests that he had read Fries' *System of Logics* (*System der Logik*) more precisely, and understood Fries' thought better than previously thought. Hegel referred to Fries' philosophy in a manuscript titled "Note on Fries" (*Notiz zu Fries*),[20] which was supposed to be a draft of a letter he sent to Niethammer in 1811.

12 Introduction

In these materials (especially the "Note on Fries"), Hegel summarized his interpretation of Fries' doctrine in the first edition of the *System of Logic*, and described his objections to it. The "Note on Fries" suggests that Hegel's comprehension of Fries' philosophy – at least regarding Fries' thoughts on logic – was quite accurate. This is most clearly exemplified by Hegel's comment on the structure of Fries' logic: "Fries [...] classified the doctrine of the concepts and judgments (species) into anthropological logic."[21] Concerning this comment, the editor of the "Note on Fries" claims that Hegel made a mistake, explaining that "Fries classified the doctrine of the concepts and judgments not into anthropological logic, but into pure, general logics, despite Hegel's claim."[22]

In fact, the first edition of Fries' *System of Logic* does not explicitly exhibit the structure of Fries' logic. He reorganized the table of contents in the second edition to show this structure more explicitly, but the structure itself was consistent (for the most part) between these two editions. The structure of Fries' logic is as follows:

1. Pure general logic.
    1.1.1 Anthropological logic.
    1.1.2 Theory of concepts and judgments.
    [...]
  1.2 Philosophical logic.
    1.2.1 Analytic cognition.
      [...]
  [...]
2 Applied logic.

This structure shows that, although Hegel referred to the first edition of Fries' book, he succeeded in grasping the structure of Fries' logic, unlike the editor of the "Note on Fries." In addition, when Hegel referred to Fries' thought, he did not make much of the role of empirical psychology. Hegel's reading note on Fries shows that Hegel understood Fries' philosophy better than previously suggested. Thus, without knowledge of Fries' philosophy, it is difficult to comprehend not only Hegel's reception of Fries but also his rival conception of philosophy, which he attempted to articulate in these materials.

1.2.3.3 Kitaro Nishida's understanding of Fries' philosophy

Fries' philosophy was often referenced by modern Japanese philosophers, especially Kitaro Nishida (1870–1945), a prominent Japanese philosopher and a founding member of the Kyoto school. Nishida referred to Fries and Friesian philosophy in his university lecture series, "Introduction to Philosophy," which he gave every year from 1910 to 1928 at Kyoto University.[23] According to Masaaki Kohsaka, an editor of "Introduction to Philosophy," the content of each lecture remained consistent for this entire period.[24] In the lecture series, Nishida examined Fries' standpoint in a section titled "Philosophy and Religion."[25] What he examined was not empirical psychology in relation to Fries' philosophy, but rather the conception of belief that Fries developed in *Knowledge, Belief, and Aesthetic Sense*.[26] Here, Fries classified the modes of cognition into knowledge (*Wissen*), belief (*Glaube*), and aesthetic sense (*Ahndung*), following the classification of Kant's concept of conviction (*Überzeugung*) or the distinction between Kant's three critiques on the basis of his methodological argument. Nishida examined Fries' argument by comparing it with Kant's classification of conviction, and illuminated its differences from Schleiermacher's standpoint.

In 1910, in a lecture at Kyoto University titled "Study of Religion,"[27] Nishida more precisely examined Fries' conception of belief in relation to the problem of religion. In this lecture, Nishida summarized Fries' philosophy and identified the Neo-Friesian school, including Leonard Nelson, Wilhelm Bousset, and Rudolf Otto, as one of the important streams of thought in the contemporary study of religion.[28] Moreover, Nishida examined Fries' conception of religion in light of his classification of modes of cognition, and emphasized its similarity to Schleiermacher's thought.[29] Nishida's precise explanation of Fries' philosophy suggests that Fries may have had much more influence than is usually credited to him on Nishida's comprehension of the history of philosophy, as well as on Nishida's formulation of his own views.

1.2.3.4 Conclusion

This chapter has examined the historical reception of Fries' philosophy as a typical example of how the historical framework of German idealism can be reconsidered.

First, the chapter described the process through which Fries' philosophy came to be regarded as psychologism. It then examined references to Fries' philosophy, made both by his contemporaries and by a Japanese philosopher, which show that they comprehended Fries' philosophy better than previously believed.

The unfortunate schematization of Fries' philosophy as psychologism in today's scholarship is a typical and illuminating example of the limitations and one-sidedness of the canonical history of philosophy, and of the framework of German idealism which Hegelian and Neo-Kantian philosophers created.

Notes

1. Whitehead [1929], p. 65.
2. Fukutani [2009], p. vii.
3. At this point, one should note another negative aspect of Fries' attitude: The anti-Semitism of the National Socialist party led by Adolf Hitler. Fries' works in his later period include anti-Semitic text, which should be severely criticized whether or not the sources are Social Nationalist. Such criticism, however, requires heavy philological examination in an independent research project. In contrast, this book focuses on the problem of philosophical methodology from a viewpoint that emphasizes Fries' influence on the later period. It is only Fries' argument concerning philosophical methods that had a significant influence on that period. A precise reconstruction of the history of 19th-century German philosophy requires reference to Fries' philosophical method, and scholarship on its formation and reception has generally ignored his political attitudes. In fact, Fries' political attitudes did not influence the formation of the Friesian school or the Neo-Friesian school. For example, Matthias Jacob Schleiden, a member of the Friesian school, influenced contemporaneous education through his counter-critique of anti-Semitism. Core members of the Neo-Friesian school, including Leonard Nelson, had Jewish roots. These facts are not valid as apologies for Fries' anti-Semitic attitude. However, this book will confirm that it is through his work on the problem of philosophical methods that Fries influenced the posterior period.
4. Beiser [2014], p. 11.
5. Ibid.
6. Ibid., p. 11f.
7. Beiser [2014], pp. 4, 53.
8. The *New or Anthropological Critique of Reason* (*Neue oder anthropologische Kritik der Vernunft*, 1828/1831) is a revised edition of the *New Critique of Reason*.
9. Fries' biography is detailed in Beiser [2014], p. 27ff.
10. Hayakawa [1986] summarizes the reception of Fries' philosophy in terms of his evaluation as a psychologistic philosopher. The outline of this chapter is based on Hayakawa [1986].
11. Hayakawa [1986], p. 5f.
12. Fischer [1862], p. 7.
13. Beiser [2014], p. 32.
14. Fischer [1862], p. 17.
15. Hayakawa [1986], p. 8.
16. Liebmann characterizes the philosophy of Fichte, Schelling, and Hegel as the idealist way (Liebmann [1865], p. 70) and Fries' philosophy as an empiricist way (ibid., p. 140).
17. Hayakawa [1986], p. 9.
18. Hatfield [1990], p. 111.
19. GW14, p. 9.
20. GW12, p. 311ff.
21. GW12, p. 312.
22. GW12, p. 357.
23. Nishida [2004a].

24 Fujita [2004], p. 641.
25 Nishida [2004a], pp. 182–194.
26 Ibid., p. 191ff.
27 Nishida [2004b].
28 Ibid., p. 36.
29 Ibid., p. 61ff.

2 Jakob Friedrich Fries' philosophy

2.1 Fries' conception of a critique of reason

2.1.1 Fries' methodological standpoint in philosophy

This chapter addresses Fries' philosophy, especially his philosophical method. As the previous chapter noted, it is characteristic of Fries' philosophy that he located the point of Kant's critical philosophy in the *method* of philosophy. From this viewpoint, Fries thematizes the process of philosophizing which precedes the philosophy itself and its methodology. He does so by criticizing German idealism from a methodological viewpoint. Fries' main book, the *Critique of Reason*, is a praxis of this process. Why, then, must Fries problematize how philosophy is done with a critique of reason? What kind of method supports Fries' standpoint? In fact, Fries' critique of reason consists of both (i) a reconsideration of the *method* of philosophizing and (ii) a praxis of philosophizing itself (the *content* of philosophizing). This chapter examines (i) the method of philosophizing, and reveals the main conception of what the critique of reason presupposes methodologically. This examination addresses why Fries focuses on the method of philosophy and in what sense the role of empirical psychology should be emphasized.

First, the chapter overviews the problem of the method of philosophy. Second, it examines previous critiques of Fries and answers them by showing how his own standpoint developed. Third, it examines how Fries formed his philosophical method in relation to his confrontation with Fichte and Schelling. Finally, this chapter addresses key concepts of Fries' philosophy with respect to its formation.[1]

2.1.1.1 Introduction to Fries' philosophy

2.1.1.1.1 OUTLINE OF FRIES' CRITIQUE OF REASON

2.1.1.1.1.1 The method of philosophizing This section addresses Jakob Friedrich Fries' conception of a "critique of reason" and reveals the way in

DOI: 10.4324/9781003406006-2

which his philosophical method ensures the apodicticity of philosophical cognition. Fries' philosophy is principally based on Immanuel Kant's method of the critique.[2] As Fries adopts much from the grounds of Kant's critical philosophy, he emphasizes the finitude of human cognition. He approves of Kant, as Kant thematized the *method* of philosophy[3] in order to attain philosophical cognition within this constraint, and also to make philosophy a science that must be open to everyone.[4] Fries emphasizes philosophy's character as a *systematic science*:

> Philosophical cognition is not something that must be investigated and newly learned by a particular person, but rather every human possesses it and adapts it daily in all thinking. [...] Mostly unconsciously and without caring, every human adopts philosophical truths without any difficulty. If, however, some people compare their ideas [*Meinungen*] to each other, they will easily stay in contradiction, no matter how they deal with their opinion of the nature of the things, ethical behavior in life, or truths of religion. Then, if we attempt to build a consensus [*verständigen*] about these issues with each other, we find that our judgment in all things starts from certain general presuppositions about nature, ethical life, and belief [...]. Generally, the component of philosophical truths certainly lies in every spirit in the same way, and only their general scientific expression can be disputed.
>
> (SM, p. 89)

Fries thinks, then, that every human already possesses philosophical cognition and then "adapts it daily in all thinking." Fries accordingly locates the task of philosophy in the clarification of the general presuppositions that construct our philosophical cognition. He gives causality as an example:

> For example, every human presupposes that every event has its cause, although philosophers might still dispute its possibility and correct expression. However, we are in doubt, even in the case of the most evident claims, as soon as we begin to consider the claims generally in a philosophical way.
>
> (SM, p. 90)

It is not the philosophical cognition we already possess that should be sophisticated in philosophizing, then, but rather the "philosophical way." Fries claims that the art of philosophizing (*Kunst zu philosophieren*)[5] should first be learned in order to philosophize. He therefore applauds Kant, who thematized and examined the art of philosophizing. Fries diagnoses his contemporaneous situation as follows:

> Then [because Kant already examined the way of philosophizing], must philosophy be already elevated to the rank of an evident science, and can an acknowledged and irreversible system be exhibited? [...] The answer to this question can be as follows: after the influence of the critique of reason, regarding the result of philosophical investigations, the agreement of German academicians has been found. However, the investigations themselves are just as disputed as in another period.
> (SM, p. 123; cf. RFS, p. 276)

Fries claims that philosophy as a science has not yet been established. He finds the cause of this in the hidden errors of Kant's own critique of reason, and its expansion in the thinking that came after Kant. Fries therefore claims that the critique of reason must be newly thematized.

The point of Fries' critique of his contemporaneous situation is a negation of the highest principle in philosophy. He examines Reinhold's standpoint as an example of this highest principle, and claims:[6]

> Among the philosophers who are most known, it was Reinhold who, as he intended to gain the unity of the Kantian system, determined the rationalist preoccupation again under the formula below: It may be the purpose of all theoretical science and speculation to deduce all our knowledge from a highest principle. This principle was supposed to be a basic proposition in a logical sense at first, but it was converted into one with a metaphysical sense, and became the idea of the universe and godhood. [...] However, a human can grasp or comprehend neither the essence of godhood nor the essence of things from it.
> (NKV, I, p. XXII; NaKV, I, p. 16)

Fries denies, then, that lower cognitions can be deduced from the highest principle in such a way. He points out that the highest principle stated by German idealists like Reinhold is a result of illegitimate abstraction and is therefore without foundation as a philosophical principle. Fries also regards the immediate cognition of the absolute[7] and the immediate highest knowledge of intellectual intuition[8] as results of the same failure. Instead of those failed principles, Fries thematizes the art of philosophizing.

2.1.1.1.1.2 Adopting the regressive method To examine the art of philosophizing, Fries starts from the standpoint of ordinary experience[9] – in other words, ordinary opinions (*gemeine Beurteilungen*) in daily life.[10] According to Fries, we always have opinions (*Beurteilunngen*) regarding truth, goodness, and beauty.[11] By analyzing these opinions, therefore, he attempts to reveal the claims that ground them[12] as general presuppositions.

> Success in the formation of philosophy is based on the *analyzing way of thought* [*der zergliedende Gedankenlauf*], the regressive methods, which elevate from the particular to the general, and therefore seek the expression of general ground truths for the first time.
>
> (SM, p. 91)

Fries makes the following claim about opinions in daily life:

> Therefore, we should always follow the method of elevating regressively from the particular to the more general, from the result to its next ground [*Grund*]. Then we get the first certain thing, which is then our foundation, from the opinions of daily life.
>
> (SM, p. 99)

As seen here, Fries calls his method the "analyzing way of thought." According to Fries, the first task of philosophy is to identify fundamental claims (*Grundbehauptungen*) through the method of analyzing philosophical opinions that arise in life.[13] He also calls this analytical method "abstraction." The fundamental claims here mean philosophical cognition, and Fries regards this as a method of grounding (*Grundlegung*) in Kant's philosophy. In addition, this method starts from the particular and achieves the general regressively, in what Fries calls the "regressive method." The regressive method is also called the "analytic method," in contrast to Reinhold's "synthetic method," which starts from the highest principle and deduces lower principles from the highest. The concept of the analytic and synthetic here derives from Kant's usage of these words in the *Prolegomena*[14] (AA, IV, p. 263), *Grounding for the Metaphysics of Morals* (AA, IV, p. 392), and *Critique of Practical Reason* (AA, V, p. 10).

However, the process of finding the fundamental claims has a particular character. Fries explains this characteristic by contrasting it with intuition.[15] According to Fries, when engaging in intuition or perception we not only intuit the external object, but also are immediately conscious of intuiting it. When we arrive at an opinion, however, we are not always conscious of the general laws under which the opinion belongs.

> All our cognition is included either in intuition or in judgment. Intuition is the cognition of which we are conscious immediately. We see and hear, for example – and simultaneously we know that, and what, we

see and hear. To the contrary, our judgments use reflection in order to elevate this particular perception to a full experience of our cognitions. In our judgments we become *mediately* conscious of what we cognize and know, without perceiving it immediately in us. Consequently, every human cognizes many mathematical and philosophical laws, and judges and behaves in accordance with them, without being conscious of knowing them. We find these laws in us again through acquiring mathematics and philosophy scientifically for the first time. Therefore whoever finds a change seeks a cause, for example, but we become conscious of the law of causality only through philosophizing.

(NKV, I, p. 70; NaKV, I, p. 106)

Fries' concept of consciousness means "the cognition of the cognition that we own,"[16] or "the inner cognition that a certain cognition is in me."[17] Therefore, his concept of being conscious means being aware of a cognition.[18] Cassirer points out that in Fries' philosophy this consciousness of cognition is "a mere re-consciousness wherein we own an existence that is already performed."[19] Therefore, while one's particular perceptions are necessarily accompanied by one's consciousness of perceiving, philosophical cognition or laws are not accompanied by consciousness of the cognition or laws themselves, although they are the presuppositions of our opinions in daily life. Philosophical cognition is a kind of cognition that is initially brought into consciousness through analysis or abstraction.[20] The role of the art of philosophizing, therefore, is to understand the obscure representations and make them clearer.[21]

2.1.1.1.1.3 The need for a theory of reason The art of philosophizing, then, means the clarification of the fundamental claim which our opinions presuppose through the analysis of these opinions. However, such an analysis itself has no limitations and can involve infinite regression. In addition, the general principle to be explained through the analysis is an unprovable proposition.[22] The status of such a general principle, its validity, and its justification should therefore be addressed.

According to Fries, finding philosophical cognition through analysis of our opinions does not mean *deducing* any general principle on the basis of them. It instead means indicating[23] that the more general proposition lies in our spirit, based on the fact that the lower propositions actually do lie there.[24]

When I follow this analyzing method, in respect to the succession from one proposition to the other, I cannot say that I have proved the deduced propositions, because here I come from the result to the ground [*Grund*], from the conclusion to the general proposition from which the conclusion is deduced. Now, however, objectively the ground is not true because the result is true, but the result is true only because the ground is true. However, when I regard something as true that exists only as a result of something else, I subjectively deduce the truth of a result as an assumption or conviction about the truth of the ground. Surely, I do not deduce the ground from the result, but rather I show that my assumption of the result presupposes the assumption of the ground.

(SM, p. 101)[25]

Fries claims that the analytical method does not prove propositions, then, but rather yields an assumption that the ground which is presupposed is true because of the truth of its results. Fries gives substance as an example:

For example, I say that every substance persists, every change has a cause, and all simultaneity is determined by the exchange of substances. Or, I judge of justice and injustice, virtue and vice, and I say above all that every reasonable existence should be treated as a purpose in itself according to its personal dignity. Or finally, I insist that there should be a God and that the will should be free. On what do I base my judgment in such cases? I recognize the laws of nature in the first case, the laws of freedom in the second, and the laws of the eternal order of things in the third, without appealing to intuition. However, these laws, of which I become re-conscious only in judgment, must exist in my reason only as immediate cognitions. I use my judgment only to become conscious of them. Hence, we can justify [*begründen*] our judgment only by showing which original cognition of reason underlies it, but without being able to put the cognition immediately next to the judgment and defend it with that judgment. Such a way to justify a principle is called its deduction.

(NKV, I, p. 283; NaKV, I, p. 342)

According to Fries, the proposition that all substances subsist is a metaphysical rule which our particular opinions presuppose. However, such a substance is not an object of our intuition, so the concept of substance is not a result of induction based on our perceptions. Rather, the opinions that presuppose the duration of substance become possible through the fact that the proposition "All substances subsist" lies in the human spirit. This analysis shows that the assumption of this general presupposition is anterior to our particular opinions.

Fries regards these general propositions which are gained through analysis as premises[26] that exist in our spirit[27] to enable lower propositions. He identifies the faculty of the spirit wherein philosophical cognition lies with

22 *Jakob Friedrich Fries' philosophy*

reason (*Vernunft*) as a mental faculty, and names his standpoint the theory of reason.[28] As shown above, the regressive method leads to the theory of reason, and is regarded as a critical method[29] that clarifies the conditions for our cognition. Therefore, philosophical investigation through analysis is called a critique of reason.

2.1.1.1.1.4 Speculation: Investigation of philosophical cognition as that of reason Fries calls the analyzing way of thought which is based on the regressive method *speculation*.

> The ordinary use of understanding adapts the concepts *in concreto*. Speculation adapts them *in abstracto*. Particular arithmetical or geometrical laws about quantity, and philosophical concepts such as cause, change, right, and wrong, arise daily in our thinking, but we only ever put them equally to use in our opinion of a particular case. To the contrary, the speculative science in mathematics and philosophy binds what is abstracted to the general. We often presuppose the constancy of particular quantities in life, but the law of constancy in general is only the object of speculation. Just like this, we often draw an inference about changes on the basis of causes in particular cases, but only speculation seeks the connection between those concepts in general.
> (NKV, I, p. 321; NaKV, I, p. 384)

Since we are not conscious of the general principles of reason, they can be clarified as the content of the immediate cognition of reason[30] through the analysis and abstraction initially called "speculation."[31] According to Fries, the imperfectness of speculation, i.e., the requirement of speculation that we do not precisely know the nature of our spirit,[32] requires the praxis of speculation, i.e., philosophizing – even today. The art of philosophizing, therefore, is identified with speculation,[33] an art with which to understand obscure representations and make them distinct, engaged in clarifying the general propositions hidden in daily life. In this sense, speculation means the operation which finds the immediate cognition of reason through analysis and abstraction.[34]

2.1.1.1.1.5 Deduction: Justification of philosophical cognition through the immediate cognition of reason As shown above, the analysis of the regressive method clarifies the general propositions our daily opinions presuppose. According to Fries, philosophical cognition as a general presupposition is a mental faculty in our reason. From this viewpoint, the analysis is called "speculation," and those propositions are validated and justified insomuch as they lie in reason (*Vernunft*). According to Fries, general propositions have validity as philosophical cognition because they are identified with the immediate cognition of reason. Such a justification is accomplished by exhibiting (*Aufweisung*) the coincidence of those propositions and the immediate cognitions of reason. Fries names this process of exhibition deduction (*Deduktion*).[35] He explains:

> [According to the cases I examined] I cognize laws of nature in the first case, laws of freedom in another case, the eternal order of things in the last case, without any requirement of intuition. However, just these laws, of which I only become conscious in judgment, must lie in my reason as an immediate cognition. I only use judgment in order to become conscious of those laws. Therefore, we can here justify our judgment by exhibiting which original cognition of reason underlies it, without any ability to state this cognition immediately next to it and defend it through that cognition. This way to justify the principle is called the *deduction* of this principle.
>
> (NKV, I, p. 283; NaKV, I, p. 342)

According to Fries, justification in general can be accomplished in three ways.[36] The first method of justification is verification (*Beweis*), which resolves (*zurückführen*) the judgment into another true judgment. This method can be applied to a verifiable judgment, i.e., a judgment that depends on another judgment. The second way is demonstration, which shows the ground (*Grund*) of the judgment in the intuition. Demonstration is applied in all the empirical sciences, and in mathematics. The last method is deduction, which exhibits the judgment as an immediate cognition of reason (*unmittelbare Erkenntnis der Vernunft*) that is applied to philosophical cognition.[37]

> Then, how do we justify the first [philosophical] principle? The answer can be found easily [...]. The truth of this principle is based on the fact that the principle coincides with the immediate cognition [of reason (*Vernunft*)]. The immediate cognition is only repeated in the principle, and it is a ground [*Grund*] for the truth of the principle.
>
> (NKV, I, p. 282; NaKV, I, p. 340)

Fries thus finds a way to justify the first principle in the exhibition of its coincidence with the immediate cognition of reason, which he calls "deduction." According to Fries, his conception of *deduction* coincides with Kant's usage of the word:

> Now, Kant had named the justification of the usage of categories with the word *deduction*. I retained this denomination because my

justification had the same purpose, and also applied similar means through correct understanding of transcendental verification.

(NaKV, I, p. XXI)

2.1.1.1.1.6 The apodicticity of philosophical cognition As shown above, the role of speculation, i.e., the art of philosophizing, is to clarify general principles as philosophical cognition and to bring that cognition into consciousness. Therefore, the highest principle can be justified by exhibiting philosophical cognition as unverifiable rules in reason.[38]

According to Fries, the immediate cognition of reason is qualified as an apodictic cognition. Certainty through intuition or perception is valid only within a particular cognition and has no further validity. Fries calls this kind of certification "assertoric." In contrast, a philosophical cognition is a general proposition that constructs the general presuppositions of particular opinions, and acquires the status of apodictic cognition, having validity for all opinions.

> Historical cognition is demonstrable, and simultaneously characteristic of the merely assertoric; it is based on a particular stimulus in sensible intuition. To the contrary, mathematical cognition is demonstrably apodictic at the same time. [...] Finally, philosophical cognition is something of which we become conscious only through reflection; it is therefore thoroughly discursive and apodictic.
>
> (NKV, I, p. 276; NaKV, I, p. 334)

The cognition with which philosophy deals, then, is apodictic cognition. The apodicticity of philosophical cognition should be based on deduction, the exhibition of its coincidence with the immediate cognition of reason. From this perspective, Fries summarizes the task of philosophy as follows:

> Philosophy is an artificial product of analysis. It attempts to abstract from the entangled concepts of ordinary experience something tenable in order to compose general and necessary laws from them.
>
> (SM, p. 107)

2.1.1.1.1.7 Critique of reason as an anthropological investigation The previous section examined the conception and method of a critique of reason. Now, the critique of reason can be regarded as a transcendental cognition in Kant's philosophy, in which transcendental cognition is related to apodictic cognition, which cannot be separated from the apriority of cognition.[39] Therefore, in Kant's philosophy the possibility of cognition *a priori* is problematized.[40] How, then, can Fries' way of philosophizing be related to cognition *a priori*?

According to Fries, although the principle of cognition is *a priori*, its cognition itself can be acquired in an empirical way. The fact that Kant regarded transcendental cognition as a kind of cognition *a priori*[41] is, for Fries, a "Kantian preoccupation."[42] Fries perceives that transcendental cognition itself need not be cognition *a priori*. Because all human cognition begins with a sensible perception, transcendental cognition itself should also be acquired empirically, but this does not mean that human cognition derives from sensible perceptions in terms of general and necessary truths.[43]

As shown above, Fries claims that the philosophical cognitions that construct the critique of reason are themselves empirical. He further claims that the critique of reason is an empirical science. He finds the object of speculation for a critique of reason in self-observation (*Selbstbeobachtung*). According to Fries, to critique reason is to find philosophical cognition as a general proposition through analysis, and to bring that cognition into consciousness. This process, Fries says, means self-cognition and self-observation.

> Therefore, every science, or every part of such a science, is a product of speculation in case it has no external experience but speculation in a strict sense, or it also has no pure intuition from which it gains its cognitions. In the latter case, the spirit is liberated, gains from itself, and observes its own cognitions. This speculation, the art of philosophizing, is therefore the art of inner self-observation; it is also the art with which to grasp the obscurer representations and make them more distinct; it is, so to speak, a sharp inner eye, through whose observation unanalyzed representations become analyzed so that order can be brought to a totality of representations.
>
> (SM, p. 105)

Fries claims that whenever he knows this or that thing, or recognizes this or that particular object, the particular fact that he does so is an object of inner experience. He regards the analysis of daily opinions as a means of investigating how philosophical cognition operates as an analysis of inner experience or inner perception, which also means inner observation. In this respect, Fries claims that the apriority of transcendental cognition[44] claimed by Kant "makes inner perception [unjustly] a cognition *a priori*."[45]

Fries also connects the critique of reason with other disciplines. He claims that this doctrine of a critique of reason that Kant called "transcendental" belongs to empirical psychology as a science of inner experience,[46] and criticizes Kant for overlooking the empirical-psychological nature of transcendental cognition.[47] Fries characterizes the critique of reason with the term "anthropological investigation."

The regressive method in philosophy leads to an anthropological investigation with the thorough subjective turn contained in this method; it changes philosophizing into the stuff of inner experience, into spiritual self-observation in accordance with experience. Therefore, we also name this regressive method the *critical method*, and the investigation itself the *critique of reason*.

(SM, p. 104)

2.1.1.1.2 CONVENTIONAL EVALUATION OF FRIESIAN PHILOSOPHY[48]

After his death, Fries' philosophy came to be regarded as psychologism, or as a psychological approach to Kant.[49] His place in the legitimate history of philosophy has consequently been forgotten.

Kuno Fischer, who was the first great opponent of Fries' philosophy and was known as a Hegelian, thematized and objected to Fries' philosophy in a lecture presented in 1862. He said that it is Fries' decisive doctrine that cognition *a priori* can be recognized in an empirical way. He clearly denied this doctrine, and rejected Fries' philosophy:

> [As Fries bases the critique of reason on empirical psychology,] now, if the critique of reason is only psychological and therefore merely empirical, how can the objects of the critique's insight be *a priori*?[50] [...]
>
> Fries objects as follows: What the critique of reason investigates is *a priori*, but the investigation itself is *a posteriori*. The object of its cognition is *a priori*; its cognition is itself empirical. [...]
>
> And just here is the πρῶτον ψεῦδος [first mistake] in Friesian philosophy. What is *a priori* can never be recognized *a posteriori*.
>
> Anyway, I do not know the distinction between the *a priori* and *a posteriori* without relation to our cognition. I do not understand how something *a priori* can exist [*sein*] while being independent of cognition. And I do not understand how a cognition *a priori* is supposed to be in ourselves which is known only by experience.
>
> (Fischer [1862], p. 18)[51]

Otto Liebmann followed Fischer's conclusion[52] and criticized Fries' philosophy as "no improvement [on Kantian philosophy], but only a retrogression to Locke."[53] Wilhelm Windelband also accepted Liebmann's appraisal, asserting that Fries' philosophy was an attempt to translate a critical principle of human reason's self-cognition into the vocabulary of empirical psychology.[54]

With this estimation, Fries' philosophy disappeared behind the orthodox genealogy of the history of German philosophy in the 19th century.

2.1.1.2 Response from a Friesian standpoint

2.1.1.2.1 RESPONSE BY LEONARD NELSON[55]

This section next reconsiders the accusation of psychologism from the standpoint of Fries' own philosophy. Leonard Nelson finds its solution in a distinction between *critique* and *metaphysics*. Fries claims throughout his work, in agreement with Kant, that metaphysics consists of cognition *a priori* – in other words, apodictic cognition.[56] However, a critique that investigates cognition *a priori* can be fulfilled in an empirical way. In his earliest work, dating back to 1798, Fries bases this distinction on another: Between the *object* of critique and the *content* of it.

> Hence, it is the business of transcendental critique to find the nature [*Inbegriff*] of our cognition *a priori* and reduce it to its principles. Now, the investigation of what kind of cognitions *a priori* we possess, and how, obviously belongs to a kind of psychological cognition in totality. [...] The object [*Gegenstand*] of transcendental critique is cognitions *a priori*; however, its content is at most *empirical* cognitions. The judgments which constitute the contents of critique are only *assertoric*; *apodictic* judgments belong to the object of critique.[57]
>
> (VePM, p. 182)

Nelson emphasizes this distinction, and finds the essence of Fries' deduction in it. He answers Liebmann's objection by explaining that the contents of critique can be empirical, and do not entail denying the possibility of cognition *a priori*.[58]

Nelson additionally emphasizes the character of Fries' deduction to answer Fischer's objection. He claims that Fischer regarded the relation between content and object as a logical relation of verification (*Beweis*) between ground (*Grund*) and consequence. However, Fries does not regard it as verification, but rather calls it deduction. Contrary to Fischer's view, the content of critique can still be empirical.[59]

However, Nelson's answer is not successful. Fischer did not deny the justification of this distinction because he considered it to be based on the relation between ground and consequence; he denied the possibility of that distinction itself on which Nelson's answer is based, because such a distinction implies an existence independent of our cognition. Hence, Fischer's objection is concerned with the validity of deduction itself. Nelson's answer is not a refutation of Fischer's objection, but rather, only a denial of it.[60]

2.1.1.2.2 RESPONDING IN ANOTHER WAY[61]

It is possible to find another solution in Fries' thought itself. In fact, he himself ceases to draw such a distinction after 1798. The critique of reason means the *method* of philosophy. However, the critique as a method itself has two aspects: (i) The study of the method itself and (ii) the adaptation of the method. (i) The study deals with the methodology of critique, i.e., how the philosophizing or critique should be carried out, and on which presuppositions this method would be based in relation to the mental faculties. (ii) The adaptation deals with the philosophical cognitions acquired through philosophizing, which constitute the presuppositions of our opinions, or the conditions of our experience in a wider sense. This distinction takes the place of that used in 1798, and corresponds to the distinction in contents between the first book and the second and third books of the *New Critique of Reason*. As the critique is based on such a distinction, Fries asserts the *apriority* and *apodicticity* of philosophical cognition.[62] This distinction is based on the concept of *opinions* (*Beurteilungen*) as an object of philosophizing, and on a precise distinction between *reason* (*Vernunft*) and *understanding* (*Verstand*), one which arose after 1798.

2.1.1.2.2.1 Turning from an empiricist standpoint by focusing on opinions[63] In his chapter of 1798 and his first book, *Reinhold, Fichte, and Schelling* (1803), Fries adopts the analytical method.[64] However, he mentions that we must start from ordinary experience (*gemeine Erfahrung*), through observing which philosophical cognitions can be found[65] that belong to reason and are valid for the condition of our experience. From this standpoint, Fries opposes his theory mainly to dogmatism.[66]

On the contrary, since the *New Critique of Reason*, Fries finds the object of the analyzing operation in *opinions in daily life* (*Beurteilung im alltäglichen Lebens*).[67] Opinions are distinguished from mere experience, or so-called sense data, because these opinions already include cognition in the shape of representations' real relations (*reele Verhältnis*),[68] which are not included in sensible intuitions[69] but have arisen from another of our mental faculties.[70] Opinions are also distinguished from logical judging (*urteilen*) because logical judging excludes cognitive contents and is only valid for the mere *form* of re-cognition.[71] This change in the analyzing operation's object made Fries' standpoint distinct from dogmatism and empiricism.[72] He identifies the purpose of philosophizing with analyzing opinions to find the philosophical cognition that constitutes the presuppositions of *all our opinions*.[73] In this sense, Fries' investigation of philosophical cognition is not only an investigation of the sort characterized as an empiricist standpoint; rather, the central point of Fries' philosophy lies in his focus on "opinion" (*Beurteilung*).

2.1.1.2.2.2 Distinction between reason and understanding

The above distinction is based on the other distinction between two mental faculties, reason (*Vernunft*) and understanding (*Verstand*), and on two lines of thought which are thematized in Fries' second philosophical book, the *System of Philosophy as an Evident Science*, published in 1804. This section examines the division of mental faculties which the critique of reason presupposes.

As shown above, the critique of reason consists of an investigation of philosophical cognition through analysis of our opinions, the exhibition of coincidence between them, and the immediate cognition of reason. This process contains two parts:

(i) A process of speculation, i.e., the operation of investigating the immediate cognition of reason through analysis.
(ii) An object of investigation: Philosophical cognition as an immediate cognition of reason.

Fries attributes these to (i) understanding and (ii) reason. Philosophical cognition that constructs the presuppositions of opinions belongs to reason as a mental faculty; this is distinguished from understanding, which fulfills the analyzing operation with arbitrary reflection through logical form. This distinction between mental faculties is peculiar when compared to contemporary German philosophy.[74]

According to Fries, human cognition consists of receptivity or sensationality (*Empfänglichkeit*), as a faculty to receive sensation, and spontaneity or self-activity (*Selbsttätignkeit*) as a faculty for applying categories to the received sensations. Fries calls the former "sense" (*Sinn*)[75] and the latter "reason" (*Vernunft*).[76] He says that reason is connected with sense,[77] and that all cognition is formed through the unity and connections[78] made by the immediate self-activity of reason.[79]

Understanding, in contrast, is defined as a faculty of reflection, employing arbitrary representation. Understanding brings our philosophical cognition into consciousness by reflecting it in a concept (*Begriff*) and judgment (*Urteil*). Judgment here is distinguished from ordinary opinions (*gemeine Beurteilung*). While opinions are supposed to include philosophical cognition as their presupposition, judgment means a mere logical form, and therefore belongs to understanding and does not include philosophical cognition.

The task of philosophizing is to clarify the fundamental claim presupposed by our opinions through analysis of them (which is valid as Kant's grounding), which Fries names the analyzing way of thought. According to Fries, the agent of the analyzing way of thought, i.e., philosophizing, is identified with understanding as a mental faculty.[80]

> Therefore, our main task [here] may be to exhibit the faculty of reflection as a necessary condition of our cognition, in the sense that we can achieve consciousness of our own immediate cognitions only through the faculty of reflection. Now, what is observed through reflection is above all the connection and unity in our cognition. The observing faculty is the faculty of arbitrary representing, which uses comparison, abstraction, and analysis in order to form concepts and apply them in judgment.
>
> (NKV, I, p. 207; NaKV, I, p. 257)

The fundamental claim as an object of investigation for the analyzing way of thought is a general proposition which our daily opinions presuppose. This fundamental claim is regarded as a philosophical cognition insomuch as it both has any ground within neither experience nor pure intuition and is validated and justified by exhibiting its coincidence with the immediate cognition of reason (which Fries calls deduction). According to Fries, reason is a faculty of synthetic unity. Our cognition includes the necessary unity and connection made by reason, and reason's forms of connection[81] provide the real relations[82] in our experience. Fries names these relations "categories." From this viewpoint, the investigation of philosophical cognition and its deduction is now redefined as an investigation of categories and the deduction of those categories.

However, while a category lies in our immediate cognition[83] as its presupposition, that category is not brought into consciousness. Therefore, the categories as the immediate cognition of reason can be brought into consciousness only through thoughts taking such forms as concepts and judgments, which the understanding uses.[84]

> [...T]he immediate spontaneity of reason is the thing wherein we unchangeably own the unity in the necessary truths. The arbitrarily active understanding is only the higher faculty of self-cognition, through which we become conscious of the activity of that immediate spontaneity of reason which every reason contains, but of which consciousness can be obtained only artificially in the formation of thinking. The arbitrary self-activity in thinking belongs to this formation of consciousness; the original [ursprünglich] spontaneity of reason belongs to cognition with necessity itself. [...] And as its result I see how the logical forms of judgment belong to the reflection which observes reason, and the categories belong to the synthesis in reason itself.
>
> (GPh, II, S. 600f)

The whole objective synthetic unity of apperception is rather the original form of unity and necessity in terms in the immediate cognition of reason itself, and not only in the reflecting understanding. The objective synthetic unity of our intuition of the world in space and time, and the objective synthetic unity that I think through the form of judgment (e.g., in the law of causation as a general and necessary natural law), are determined not through the unity of self-consciousness, but simply through the unity of reason.

(GPh, II, p. 601f.)

As shown above, while cognition of understanding is mediated (*mittelbar*) because philosophical cognition is brought into consciousness for the first time by being brought there *through the logical form of understanding*,[85] cognition of reason must immediately belong to reason without consciousness.[86] As such immediate cognition of reason is always obscure (*dunkel*) and unconscious,[87] cognition of reason must be distinguished from intuitive cognition of sensibility,[88] which is already evident. What philosophizing must do is show that these presuppositions are the immediate cognition of reason.

From this perspective, reason is determined as a faculty engaged in the categories that enable the synthetic unity which forms the real relationship.[89] Understanding, in contrast, is determined as a faculty of reflection in general.[90] Understanding includes only valid forms of thinking[91] and is engaged in the logical relationship, and must therefore take the content of philosophical cognition from reason. In this sense, the agent of the analyzing way of thought, i.e., philosophizing, is identified with understanding. Accordingly, Fries calls understanding the superior faculty of self-cognition.[92]

> Understanding, faculty of thinking, faculty of reflecting, must be distinguished carefully from the faculty of immediate cognition, from reason. The understanding is the superior faculty of self-cognition, which is tasked to lead us into consciousness of the cognition which we have in us. Therefore, thinking does not by nature provide new cognitions in our spirit, but only presupposes that the cognitions are given to us, and the understanding will observe these cognitions. Therefore, the understanding should bring into self-observation above all the cognitions that are not intuitive for itself. This non-intuitive faculty, however, is *pure reason* in the strict sense; hence the understanding stands with this faculty of reason in a close relationship, and serves reason in order to bring the representations of reason into consciousness.

(SL, p. 92)

2.1.1.2.2.3 Distinction between the memorized line of thought and the logical line of thought
As shown above, Fries bases the condition for philosophizing on the distinction between understanding and reason. From this distinction, Fries draws two lines of thought.[93] He defines them as follows:

> The consideration of inner sense has shown by nature for the first time the standpoint from which our anthropological investigations must start. It has shown the point from which only we can observe us ourselves. Therefore, it is the empirical state of mind, occurring immediately in the intuition. In this state of mind, at first, we have considered the activity belonging to the cognition of the intuition of sense, to which we are necessarily obligated in sensation. Now, we call those which [...] belong to the empirical state of mind, except some representations [i.e., spontaneity and sensible intuitions], in general *line of thought*; it is therefore something from which our further observations must be borrowed.
>
> (NKV, I, p. 93; NaKV, I, p. 134)

As shown above, the line of thought means the empirical state of mind except for the intuition of sense, i.e., such activities as recollection, inner perception, imagination or thinking, conceptualizing, and judging. Fries distinguishes the line of thought in two ways: The line of memorized thought (*gedächtnismäßiger Gedankenlauf*) and the line of logical thought (*logischer Gedankenlauf*).[94] Fries notes that memory, inner perception of representations, recollection, and the peculiar law of imagination[95] belong to the memorized line of thought. Meanwhile, the logical line of thought consists of arbitrary reflection, served by the mediation of logical cognition with concepts, judgment, inference, and science.[96] The distinction between these two lines of thought corresponds to the distinction between reason, connected with sensibility, and understanding.

> According to time, the history of our cognition begins with the affection of sensation just because reason is connected with sense. Its activity is stimulated through this connection, but once this activity is in order, the working of the imagination appears in accordance with inner laws, and with that the working of the understanding appears. Therefore, we observe at first our state of sensation in ourselves, and then we consider the line of thought that accompanies them and from which we must learn all other laws of cognition.
>
> (NKV, I, p. 47f.; NaKV, I, p. 82)

According to Fries, the art of philosophizing, i.e., speculation by the understanding as an analyzing way of thought, is enabled by the logical line of thought.

However, this arbitrariness [of the logical line of thought] is not the only thing that accompanies our representations in the logical line of thought. With this arbitrariness, the logical way of representation appears in particular, i.e., the mediate way of cognition through concepts within judgments, according to which this line of thought is named, and on which the re-consciousness of cognitions of the superior faculty of cognition is based.

(NKV, I, p. 94; NaKV, I, p. 135)

As shown above, Fries distinguishes the memorized line of thought from the logical line of thought, and attributes reason to the former and understanding to the latter. His aim here is to establish a condition in which understanding, as a faculty of arbitrary reflection, accomplishes arbitrary reflection independently of reason, while reflection of the understanding requires its content to be philosophical cognition as the immediate cognition of reason.

The art of philosophizing, i.e., speculation, has its task in the analysis of inner observation or inner perception, of which the memorized line of thought consists. Fries attributes the *topos* of speculation to the memorized line of thought, and defines speculation as an arbitrary determination of thinking[97] that the understanding, as a faculty of reflection, accomplishes through concepts and judgment, enabled by the logical line of thought. What gives judgment its forms is *logic* as a discipline. Logic is therefore the form of thinking that determines the logical line of thought, through which understanding brings philosophical cognition into consciousness. Therefore, logic determines the form of philosophy as a science.[98] In this sense, Fries calls the logic the "ground and propaedeutic of all the other sciences."[99]

2.1.1.2.3 THE ROLE OF PSYCHOLOGY: AGAINST PSYCHOLOGISM[100]

As seen already, Nelson's understanding of Fries' philosophical standpoint is different from Fries' own. Such a difference also appears in their understanding of the role of psychology. Nelson regards Fries' critique as psychological because it is concerned with reason as a mental faculty. In this respect, he defines psychology in the wider sense: A science of inner experience.[101]

However, Fries' standpoint differs from Nelson's. According to Fries, the act of having opinions (*beurteilen*) belongs to inner experience; in this sense, he admits that the analytical process could be a matter of empirical psychology.

> Every particular fact that I know this or that thing, that I recognize this or that particular object, is an object of inner experience. Hence, there is a twofold standpoint of observation. At first every cognition corresponds [*zukommen*] to an object which should be recognized in that cognition, and then, if I should be able to judge [*urteilen*] anything about that cognition, I must be conscious of the cognition itself again [*wieder bewußt*] for the first time.
> (NKV, I, p. XXXVII; NaKV, I, p. 37)[102]

Hence, the opinions (*Beurteilungen*) belong to inner experience, and to inner perception[103] in the sense that we must be able to become *conscious* of them.[104] In this respect, Fries also recommends using the term "philosophical anthropology" instead of "psychology," to avoid misunderstanding.[105] He makes use of the products of psychology for philosophizing,[106] but carefully restricts its role to avoid falling into psychologism.

2.1.1.3 Conclusion

Fries' philosophy is based on the view that cognition *a priori* can be acquired in an empirical way. From this standpoint he adopts a regressive or analytic method, and locates the method of philosophizing in the process of analyzing ordinary opinions in daily life, in order to reveal the philosophical cognition that constitutes the general presuppositions which underlie those opinions. Such an operation aims to exhibit philosophical cognition as the immediate cognition of reason, i.e., deduction. From this standpoint, Fries takes much of empirical psychology and philosophical anthropology.

However, his philosophy has been considered unjustly to be psychologism, since Kuno Fischer claimed that cognition *a priori* can be only recognized *a priori*, and criticized Fries' philosophy by highlighting his emphasis on psychology. Leonard Nelson tried to answer this objection by emphasizing the distinction, which Fries proposes in his earliest work, between the object and content of critique.

However, Fries himself answers the objection in another way in his *New Critique*, which supersedes his earliest work. First, he avoids empiricism by finding the object of philosophizing in opinions, instead of in experience. Second, he confirms the apodicticity of philosophical cognition by finding the agent of philosophizing in the understanding, as a faculty of arbitrary reflection which brings that cognition into consciousness through its logical form, and is distinguished from reason, which possesses immediate cognition. Fries carefully restricts the role of psychology itself.

It can be seen that Fries investigated his way into metaphysics as a system of knowledge that is composed of apodictic philosophical cognition *a priori*, while remaining within the constraint of criticism in a Kantian sense. He seemed to indicate another way forward, during the development of Kantian philosophy in the 19th century, when compared to German idealism.

2.1.2 Formation of the method of philosophy: Confronting Fichte and Schelling

This section examines the development of Fries' method of philosophy in accordance with the evolution of his critique of Fichte and Schelling.

The previous section showed how Fries formed his standpoint by developing his philosophical method. The development of his thought is based on his critique of contemporaneous philosophers, the German idealists. This attitude is consistent from his earliest paper, "On the Relationship of Empirical Psychology to Metaphysics" (1798), to his main book, the *New Critique of Reason* (1807). However, the specific opponent changes with the period of philosophical development. In his earliest paper, the point of critique consists of analyzing Fichte's standpoint. Yet in his main book, the *New Critique of Reason*, Fries radicalizes his critique of Schelling's standpoint, while the critique of Fichte remains.

How, then, had this change of target from Fichte to Schelling occurred? This book finds the cause of this transition in the development of Fries' methodological standpoint. Accordingly, this section first examines Fries' critique of Fichte to reveal the methodological standpoint of Fries' philosophy in its earliest period. Second, it describes that standpoint's transition between his earliest paper and the *New Critique of Reason*, which created the shift after which Fries criticizes Schelling's standpoint rather than Fichte's.

2.1.2.1 Fries' standpoint regarding psychology and metaphysics and his object of critique

2.1.2.1.1 VIEWS ON PSYCHOLOGY AND METAPHYSICS

As the previous section showed, Fries' starting point in the formation of his philosophy lies in adopting the analytic method. In his earliest paper, he distinguishes philosophical cognition from both mere sensation and mathematical cognition by indicating that metaphysical cognition is completely based on concepts.[107] In addition, he locates the starting point of philosophy in confusion about a particular thought,[108] claiming that these concepts can be grasped only obscurely and through experience, the same as in ordinary thinking.[109] From this perspective, Fries finds his standpoint in the regressive[110] or analytic method,[111] by claiming that the first investigation from which only metaphysics departs must be based on an analysis which is necessarily in accordance with the regressive method.[112] The analytic method means the method elevating regressively from the particular to the more general, from the results to the next ground.[113] The consistent insight of those views lies in the fact that every human possesses philosophical cognition and adapts that cognition daily in all thinking.[114] As shown above, Fries starts the formation of his philosophy by adopting this regressive or analytic method.

Simultaneously, in his earliest paper Fries identifies the object of philosophy in ordinary experience, claiming that a transcendental critique starts from the standpoint of ordinary experience under the analytic method. In this paper, Fries assumes that philosophical cognition can be acquired through analysis of ordinary experience. In this sense, Fries' standpoint in this paper cannot be distinguished from mere empiricism.

2.1.2.1.2 THE OBJECT OF CRITIQUE IN THE EARLIEST PAPER: INTELLECTUAL INTUITION AS A TURNING POINT

As shown above, in his earliest paper, Fries locates the object of philosophizing only in ordinary experience. In this period, he distinguishes his standpoint only from dogmatism, by which he means starting from the highest principle to deduce lower principles from the higher. Fries names this the progressive or synthetic method, and finds an example in Reinhold and Fichte's standpoint; the critique of Fichte remains in the *New Critique of Reason* in order to exaggerate Fries' own standpoint. Fries criticizes Fichte by finding the point of Fichte's synthetic method in its conception of intellectual intuition. He summarizes Fichte's standpoint as follows:

> Therefore, actually in his *science of knowledge*, in accordance with the analogy with a metaphysics of inner nature, Fichte starts from the concept of a limited, internally active being (the I), and dares to deduce the whole system of philosophy with the help of inner intellectual intuition. [...] The intellectual intuition serves Fichte, as the immediate consciousness serves Reinhold, in order to introduce empirical concepts as philosophical ones from inner perception. However, our inner intuition is sensible but never intellectual; if not, we must never be able to think the non-being of the I [...].
> (VePM, p. 196)

Jakob Friedrich Fries' philosophy 37

In this earliest paper, Fries refers to Fichte's science of knowledge without naming specific texts. However, in his dissertation, on intellectual intuition, Fries problematizes the concept of intellectual intuition by referring to the *Grounding of Science of Knowledge* (1794/1795) and *An Attempt at a New Presentation of the Science of Knowledge* (1797). Commenting on the latter, Fichte summarizes his own standpoint with the term "intellectual intuition." Fries also summarizes Fichte's standpoint in the 1798 paper, interpreting it from Fries' own methodological standpoint, and then identifies Fichte's as a methodological scheme of a synthetic method. This interpretation of Fichte also remains in the *New Critique of Reason*.

As shown above, in his earliest paper Fries finds his standpoint in the regressive or analytic method, and exaggerates it by contrasting it with Fichte's conception of intellectual intuition. This opposition is the framework of Fries' earliest standpoint.

2.1.2.2 Fries' standpoint in the New Critique of Reason

2.1.2.2.1 SOPHISTICATION OF THE METHOD OF PHILOSOPHY IN THE *NEW CRITIQUE OF REASON*

In the period of the *New Critique of Reason*, Fries' philosophical method becomes more sophisticated. First, he finds the object of philosophizing not only in mere "ordinary experience," but rather in the "ordinary opinions in daily life."[115] Unlike mere experience, opinion includes the relations of representations that are not included in mere sensible intuition. In this sense, Fries' concept of opinion as the starting point of philosophy is distinguished from mere sensible intuition or sense data. It is also distinguished from logical judgments, which are only forms with which to bring philosophical cognition into consciousness.[116] With this sophistication of his method of philosophy, Fries finds the task of philosophizing in the investigation of philosophical cognition, constructing the general presuppositions which underlie our daily opinions through analysis of these opinions.

In accordance with this methodological sophistication, Fries also examines the content of the operation of this analysis. He focuses on the concept of abstraction as a means of locating philosophical cognition. While he does not refer to abstraction in his earliest paper, at the beginning of the *New Critique of Reason* Fries declares that in philosophy all things are based on regulated sharp abstraction, and he identifies his methodological point with the operation of abstraction. Fries divides the operation of abstraction into "quantitative abstraction" (also called "synthetic abstraction") and "qualitative abstraction" (also called "analytic abstraction").[117] Quantitative abstraction is a process used to extract the representation of a whole by rejecting parts of a representation. As examples, Fries mentions the concepts of specific nationalities, formed by rejecting particular differences of individuals in human groups; all representations about a certain figure, which are formed by rejecting all components outside its outlines; and the representations of space and time *in abstracto*.[118] Qualitative abstraction means an operation to extract a partial representation by separating particular characteristics as a general feature of the representation. While Fries does not note examples of this abstraction in the *New Critique of Reason*, in his previous book, *Reinhold, Fichte, and Schelling*, he mentions as examples the representations of "human," "virtue," and "black,"[119] which are valid as partial representations or general features of a "virtuous black human." Fries emphasizes the role of qualitative abstraction in philosophy:

> Through this analytic abstraction [qualitative abstraction] the representations receive the relation of a sphere and content. Analytic abstraction would surely lead the determinate forms of the logical way of representation by giving us concepts.
>
> (NKV I, p. 234f.)

Fries claims that previous philosophers overlooked this distinction between forms abstraction and wrongfully utilized quantitative abstraction, which is valid only for particular representations like space and time.[120] This insight is used in the second volume of the *New Critique of Reason* to apply his philosophical method and establish his system.

This distinction between forms of abstraction also appears in his previous book, *Reinhold, Fichte, and Schelling*. In this book Fries uses qualitative abstraction, which is also termed "Aristotelian abstraction," while quantitative abstraction is "Platonic abstraction." From this viewpoint, Fries characterizes German idealists engaged in Platonic abstraction as Platonists.[121] He claims that their philosophy has been formed through the wrongful usage of quantitative abstraction, and names Fichte and Schelling as examples of Platonists.

2.1.2.2.2 THE OBJECT OF CITIQUE IN THE *NEW CRITIQUE OF REASON*: CRITIQUE BASED ON ABSTRACTION

The development of Fries' philosophical method also changes his specific target in his critique of contemporaneous German idealists. In the *New Critique of Reason*, in addition to the regressive method, Fries also constructs his philosophical method using abstraction. In accordance with this, a new object of critique based on abstraction appears in Fries' philosophy: Schelling's philosophy.

Jakob Friedrich Fries' philosophy 39

Fries criticizes Schelling's philosophy from the viewpoint of the *method of philosophy*, most drastically in §63 of the first volume of *New Critique of Reason*. Here Fries confirms that the task of philosophy is to bring philosophical cognition into consciousness through abstraction. He sets out the concept of abstraction in §60 and classifies the different kinds of abstraction.[122] Here he finds the agent of abstraction in reflection, claiming that in philosophical cognition we become conscious through abstraction for the first time. In §63, Fries focuses on the operation of abstraction, i.e., the correct manner in which we come to a complete re-consciousness of our cognition as it is located in reason.[123]

In this respect, Fries identifies Schelling's viewpoint as an object of critique. Fries indicates that the Schellingian reasoning which divides cognition into cognition *a priori* and *a posteriori* should be rejected and is incorrect.[124] He reconfirms his view that we can perceive an apodictic law only by means of reflection,[125] and points out that Schelling's standpoint is based on the wrong process of abstraction and therefore is defective in the process of reflection.

Fries claims that Schelling's approach is to form a science "through absolute intuition rather than a detour of reflection."[126] From Fries' standpoint, Schelling, symbolized by absolute identity and indifference, dogmatically states a principle that can never be an object of our cognition, and does so in terms of the limits of that very cognition as a starting point for philosophical investigation. In other words, Schelling overlooked the distinction between discursive and intuitive cognition[127] as a point of Kant's criticism, insomuch as Schelling's approach to the formation of philosophical concepts is illegitimate. This means, according to Fries, that Schelling appeals to an intuition that humans cannot achieve: The *absolute intuition*, as Fries puts it. Based on this critique of Schelling, Fries reconfirms his view that we use the highest abstraction and reflection in order to achieve philosophy, and examines precise determinations for doing so.

As shown above, in the period of the *New Critique of Reason* Fries focuses on the nature of abstraction and on his concomitant critique of contemporaneous philosophers, principally Schelling. His multifaceted critiques appear in the second volume, in which Fries uses abstraction to form his system of philosophy. While Fries prefers to criticize Fichte's standpoint when forming his basic approach to the regressive method, he refers to Schelling's with respect to the specific manner of abstraction.

2.1.2.3 Conclusion

This section has examined the development of Fries' philosophical method. In his earliest period Fries finds the foundation of his standpoint in the regressive or analytic method, and identifies the object of his critique with Fichte's concept of intellectual intuition. In the more sophisticated *New Critique of Reason* Fries identifies the object of philosophizing as opinion, and focuses on the nature of abstraction. He criticizes Schelling's standpoint, especially when establishing his own.

This transition between targets of critique is connected to the difference between the Friesian School and Neo-Friesian School established after Fries' death. While the Friesian school is influenced by Fries' natural philosophy, developed in the second volume of the *New Critique of Reason*, and finds its counterpoint in Schelling's philosophy, the Neo-Friesian school draws its inspiration from Fries' methodological standpoint in his earliest period, and criticizes Fichte and his contemporaries by characterizing them with the term "intellectual intuition." The development of Fries' thought and his transition between targets of critique correspond to the difference between the Friesian and Neo-Friesian schools.

2.2 On the construction of a metaphysical system: From the viewpoint of the method of philosophy

This section examines the development of Fries' key concepts and the formation of his metaphysics in relation to his philosophical method. As a result of the method explained in section 2.1, Fries' metaphysics contains some features which differ from Kant's views. This section deals with the characteristics of Fries' metaphysics, including its central concepts.

This examination begins with the concept of a "feeling of truth" (*Wahrheitsgefühl*). As seen already, Fries finds the means to justify philosophical cognitions in "deduction." Simultaneously, Fries introduces the concept of a "feeling of truth," which is another criterion for the justification of philosophical cognitions. The concept of a "feeling of truth" is highly ambiguous, and performs different roles in different periods. This section traces the concept of this "feeling of truth" through the periods of development of Fries' thought, in order to reveal the role this concept plays and Fries' purpose in introducing it, i.e., the expansion of the object of philosophy.

In the period of the *New Critique of Reason*, Fries identifies the object of philosophy with the metaphysical principles of the natural sciences, such as causality or substance, and believed that ethical principles can be grasped and justified by analogy with these scientific ones. Thus, Fries does not acknowledge a role for the "feeling of truth" in the *New Critique of Reason*. In *Knowledge, Belief, and Aesthetic Sense*, however, Fries introduces a new distinction, classifying our cognition into three types:

Knowledge (*Wissen*), which is concerned with the metaphysical principles that are presupposed by (scientific) judgments regarding perceptual objects; belief (*Glaube*), which is concerned with the presuppositions of our ethical behavior; and aesthetic sense (*Ahndung*), which is concerned with judgments regarding beauty and sublimity. Fries then introduces Kant's distinction between appearances and things in themselves, and identifies the realm of "knowledge" with appearances, that of "belief" with the thing in itself, and "aesthetic sense" with the bridge between appearance and the thing in itself. In accordance with this development in his thought, Fries attempts to treat ethical principles in a different manner from metaphysical ones in his *System of Metaphysics* and *Handbook of Philosophy of Religion*.

This section next examines the concept of the thing in itself in Fries' philosophy to reveal the originality of Fries' metaphysics. That Fries acknowledges the existence of the thing in itself has been exaggerated by many researchers, from Liebmann to Beiser, as a characteristic that distinguishes Fries' standpoint from German idealists'. On the other hand, Fries denies the possibility of the thing in itself in terms of the concept of transcendental truth. This book reveals the double meaning of the "thing in itself" in Fries' philosophy, in order to resolve this contradiction and clarify his objective. When Fries denies the possibility of the thing in itself, with this concept Fries symbolizes a view that confuses appearances with things in themselves. In this context, Fries thinks of the German idealists, and attempts to criticize them by claiming the impossibility of a thing in itself. To the contrary, when Fries acknowledges the existence of the thing in itself, he renames it the "essence of things" or the "being *of things* in themselves." Here Fries redefines the "thing in itself" as the "essence of things" in order to replace this concept in his system of metaphysics, and to enable "belief" as a form of cognition to be distinct from "knowledge." In this sense, Fries characterizes his own view in comparison to his contemporaries' through his replacement of the concept of the "thing in itself."

2.2.1 Feeling of truth

2.2.1.1 Descriptions of the feeling of truth

This section addresses the role of Fries' feeling of truth (*Wahrheitsgefühl*) in relation to the development of his philosophy.[128]

As already seen, Fries claims that we have philosophical cognition without being conscious of it, and that we adopt that cognition in our ordinary opinions (*Beurteilungen*) in daily life. Fries then locates the task of philosophy in analyzing our opinions to reveal the philosophical cognition they presuppose.

How, then, can any philosophical cognition discovered through analysis be identified? While Fries mentions that the validity of philosophical cognition should be justified by reason as a mental faculty, he also claims that philosophical cognition can be identified thanks to the feeling of truth. As Fries does not provide a consistent explanation of this feeling of truth, the concept has been regarded as ambiguous in his philosophy. This section attempts to solve this problem by tracing the development of Fries' thought, and to clarify the role of the feeling of truth in his philosophy.

Fries finds the path to philosophical cognition in the feeling of truth. In his main book, the *New Critique of Reason*, he explains this concept:

> We often think something true or false, without realizing its essence, proving it, and being capable of giving a correct explanation of why we think it to be so. We find this with feeling. Hence, we have a feeling of truth that leads us frequently in our opinions but especially works as a feeling of beauty and as an ethical feeling.
>
> (NKV, I, p. 342)[129]

In the *New Critique of Reason*, Fries finds a *prima facie* means to understand philosophical cognition in the concept of the feeling of truth. Although he also relates this concept to the beauty of things and to ethical principles,[130] in the *New Critique* he does not intend to make this concept central as a means to find philosophical cognition. In fact, Fries places this chapter at the end of the first book of his *New Critique*, and he does not provide a precise explanation.[131]

Since the role of the feeling of truth is ambiguous, Fries' philosophy has often been misunderstood. Furthermore, he adopts different views regarding this concept, making its role more ambiguous still.

The following section describes the development of this concept in relation to that of Fries' thought.

2.2.1.2 The development of Fries' philosophical conception and the role of the feeling of truth

2.2.1.2.1 REINHOLD, FICHTE, AND SCHELLING

2.2.1.2.1.1 The standpoint of Reinhold, Fichte, and Schelling Fries claims throughout, in agreement with Kant, that metaphysics consists of cognition *a priori*; in other words, apodictic cognition.[132] However, the critique that investigates cognition *a priori* can be fulfilled in an empirical way. As shown in the previous section, in his earliest work, dating back to 1798,

Fries bases this distinction on another, between the *object* of critique and the *content* of it.

> Hence, it is the business of a transcendental critique to find the nature [*Inbegriff*] of our cognition *a priori* and reduce it to its principles. Now, the investigation of what kind of cognitions *a priori* we possess, and their nature, obviously belongs to a kind of psychological cognition in totality. [...] The object [*Gegenstand*] of transcendental critique is cognitions *a priori*, but its content is at most *empirical* cognitions. The judgments which constitute the contents of critique are only *assertoric*; *apodictic* judgments belong to the object of critique.[133]
> (VePM, p. 182)

In his chapter of 1798 and in his first book, *Reinhold, Fichte, and Schelling*, Fries adopts the analytic method.[134] However, he mentions there that we must start from ordinary experience (*gemeine Erfahrung*), and by doing so, find the philosophical cognition that can be found,[135] that belongs to reason, and that is valid for the condition of our experience. From this standpoint, Fries opposes his theory mainly to dogmatism.[136]

2.2.1.2.1.2 The earliest description of the Feeling of Truth in Reinhold, Fichte, and Schelling

The first use of this concept in Fries' philosophy is in his earliest book, *Reinhold, Fichte, and Schelling*. In this book Fries tries to introduce this concept to explain his views in relation to his contemporaries'. He gives the following description:

> We often think something true or false, without realizing its essence, proving it, and being capable of giving a correct explanation of why we think it to be so. Commonly we find this with feeling. However, we should not think that we depend on the perception, i.e., on the sense. It is not the sense but the understanding makes a demand. The distinction is one of whether I am going to be conscious of this judgment immediately, or whether I am conscious of judgments from which the very judgment follows. In the first case I give only my feeling as the ground of the judgment. We commonly [*im allgemeinen*] call the faculty [*Vermögen*] of judging through feelings a "feeling of truth," and we adopt it especially in the cases of ethical feeling and a feeling for beauty.
> (RFS, p. 289)

As will be seen, although Fries already identifies the originality of his thoughts about philosophizing with an emphasis on experience, he does not fully develop this thought in *Reinhold, Fichte, and Schelling*.

Although the concept of a feeling of truth is already related to ethical and aesthetic contexts, it is remarkable that Fries here refers to this concept by explaining that we *generally* call this faculty the feeling of truth. In this sense, although Fries was already beginning to grasp some ideas about this concept, it did not have its own place in his philosophy.[137]

2.2.1.2.1.3 Distinguishing three modes of cognition in Knowledge, Belief, and Aesthetic Sense While in the *New Critique of Reason* Fries thematizes the method of philosophy, at the same time he tries to make a strict distinction between modes of philosophical cognition. He tries to classify philosophical cognition into three categories: Knowledge (*Wissen*), belief (*Glaube*), and aesthetic sense (*Ahndung*). Knowledge is concerned with metaphysical principles, belief with ethical principles, and aesthetic sense with the principles of beauty.

Fries thematizes this distinction mainly in 1805's *Knowledge, Belief, and Aesthetic Sense*. In this book he finds in knowledge a way to recognize finitude, in belief a way to grasp the eternal, and in aesthetic sense a way for cognition to combine both.

> We say that belief about the eternal and about the reality of the highest goods in the eternal is the first presupposition in every finite reason [*Vernunft*]. We know [*wissen*] only of the finite through experience. However, we relate the being [*Sein*] of the finite with the idea [*Idee*] of the eternal. We presuppose the eternal [...] . This jump from knowing to believing is suspicious for everyone, and a *salto mortale* from philosophy to unphilosophy [*Unphilosophie*] for every dogmatic philosophy. [...]
>
> On the contrary, critical philosophy shows the insiders of dogmatic philosophy, clearly and distinctly, how this belief arises in the essence of reason; how all our knowledge is combined with the finite but belief grasps the eternal, and the aesthetic sense combines both the finite and the eternal, and unifies the eternal with the finite.
>
> (WGA, p. 54)

2.2.1.2.2 EXTENSION OF THE OBJECTS OF PHILOSOPHY AND CENTRALIZATION OF THE FEELING OF TRUTH

2.2.1.2.2.1 Extension of the objects of philosophy The development of a distinction between the modes of cognition results in the expansion of the object of philosophy.

As already seen, in Fries' earlier works he identifies the object of philosophy mainly with metaphysical principles that are related to natural science.

Hence the validity and limitations of these principles can be demonstrated through experience. Although in *Knowledge, Belief, and Aesthetic Sense* Fries already thematizes the distinction between the three titular modes of cognition, in the *New Critique of Reason* he does not thematically address the distinction between their natures, and he tries to treat the ethical principles (objects of belief) by analogy with metaphysical principles (objects of knowledge).

An example of such analogous treatment of metaphysical and ethical principles is found in the role of induction in Fries' philosophy. As we have already seen, he emphasizes the role of experience in philosophizing; he also regards induction as an important means to gain philosophical cognition. In the *New Critique of Reason*, Fries treats ethical principles in the same way as metaphysical ones, and emphasizes the role of induction rather than the feeling of truth, even in the context of ethics. An example is found in the following:

> The depicted reason [*Scheingrund*] for this empirical induction of morality is the same as for all empirical induction, the argument of Humian doubt: We constitute all general rules that are valid in experience, e.g., under the law of causality, for the first time through inductions.
> (NKV, III, p. 138)

Here Fries examines the validity of induction by referring to Hume's argument. It can be found here that Fries treats the induction of morality in the same way as metaphysical principles like causality.

However, after the *New Critique of Reason*, Fries comes to thematize the ethical principles independently. At the same time, he realizes that it is impossible to treat ethical principles by analogy with metaphysical ones because of the difference in their nature. It is a development and extension of the object of his philosophy that makes Fries recognize this difference. After the *New Critique of Reason*, he extends the object of philosophy to religious convictions that are related to belief and aesthetic sense.

2.2.1.2.2.2 Centralization of the feeling of truth after the System of Metaphysics In his *System of Metaphysics* from 1824, Fries begins to reconsider the importance of the feeling of truth. He thematizes the role of this concept in his philosophy in order to distinguish his own philosophy from Hume's and Jacobi's thought.[138]

> The ordinary [*gesund*] feeling of truth lets everyone follow the intuitive cognition in perception and mathematics even if there is no belief. And who would say that he has a belief that every change should have a cause? Who would say that mass should not be able to increase or

decrease in all actions of material world? The ordinary human understanding presupposes these truths through its feeling of truth in the ordinary opinions of daily life, which can be easily shown. Only in the case of religious truths – for example, in the case of belief [*Überzeugung*] that the soul is immortal or the holy will is a creator of all things – is the feeling of truth at the same time pure belief, a belief of ethical self-confidence.

(SM, p. 74)

Here it is evident that Fries recognizes this concept's specific role in the context of ethics. However, here he treats such a role as only an exceptional case; and yet he finds in that role the *prima facie* means to locate philosophical cognition, which can be justified for the first time through deduction.

The original role of this concept in an ethical context can be found in his *Handbook of Philosophy of Religion* from 1832. In this book, Fries does not treat ethical problems only by analogy with metaphysical principles, but tries to thematize ethical principles themselves and treat them in relation to religious beliefs.

> I unify the philosophy of religion and philosophical aesthetics, or the theory of beauty, into one task. On this point, regarding the intention, perhaps I agree with some theories of Schelling's school.
>
> However, in my case, the unification is not as same as that of Schelling's school, according to which religious belief might be manifested as the highest knowledge of our spirit. The unification is fulfilled because the feeling of truths of belief and aesthetic sense, as opposed to knowledge, should defend human world-teleology, and this unification should be a philosophy of feelings and show how humans' strong, radical belief [*festeste Grundüberzeugung*] about the true, the good, and the beautiful would be found in the immediate life of our feeling of truth, which is opposed to the development of scientific forms.

(R, p. 1)

In the *Handbook*, Fries draws a sharp distinction between scientific forms and ethical principles, and tries, by reconsidering the role of the feeling of truth, to distinguish his own views from those of conventional philosophers like Schelling and Jacobi. It was this development in Fries' philosophy that led him to make the concept of the feeling of truth a central part of it.

2.2.1.3 Conclusion

This section has dealt with the development of the role of the feeling of truth in Fries' philosophy. In his main book, the *New Critique of Reason*, while Fries identifies deduction as the way to justify philosophical cognition, he finds the means of locating it in the feeling of truth. Since the concept of the feeling of truth is ambiguous, Fries' philosophy has often been misunderstood.

The section examined the development of this concept in relation to that of Fries' philosophical thought. We found the first use of this concept in his first book, *Reinhold, Fichte, and Schelling*. After this book, Fries' philosophical method matured in the *New Critique of Reason*, and at the same time, he distinguished three modes of cognition in *Knowledge, Belief, and Aesthetic Sense*. These two aspects of the development of his philosophy resulted in the expansion of its object; this concept ultimately became central in the context of ethics.

As we have seen, changes in the role of this concept accompanied the development of Fries' philosophy itself. The concept of the feeling of truth does not suggest ambiguity in Fries' philosophical views, but rather the continuous development and improvement of Fries' philosophy itself.

2.2.2 The thing in itself in Fries' philosophy

2.2.2.1 The thing in itself as a problem in Fries' philosophy

2.2.2.1.1 THE THING IN ITSELF IN FRIES' PHILOSOPHY

This section considers the concept of the thing in itself in Fries' philosophy in relation to his theory of truth, in order to clarify the meaning of this concept.

Fries' philosophy has been characterized in terms of the concept of the thing in itself. Although German idealists such as Reinhold, Fichte, and Schelling attempt to exclude the concept of the thing in itself and attempt to complete Kant's philosophy, Fries does seem to acknowledge the existence of the thing in itself in some texts:

> The being of things in relation to absolute necessity is called *the being in itself*. The being of the things of nature in contrast to that is called *the being in the appearance*. Hence, *a transcendental reality of things in themselves* underlies *all empirical reality of appearance*. However, we are conscious of the transcendental reality only through negation of the restriction in our representation of appearances.
>
> (SPh, p. 246)

Through these subjective restrictions in the consciousness of our cognitions, the distinction between the *appearance and being of things in themselves*, or eternal truth, becomes thinkable.

(SM, p. 228)

Fries' acknowledgment of the thing in itself has often been thematized. Otto Liebmann regards it as Fries' significant fault. As Liebmann regards the concept of the thing in itself in Kantian philosophy as a contradiction to be eliminated, he severely criticizes and rejects Fries' philosophy.[139] In contrast, some researchers regard Fries' acknowledgment of the thing in itself as proof that he was a legitimate Kantian. According to Frederick Beiser, Fries' acknowledgment of the thing in itself here implies an emphasis on the finitude of human cognition, which distinguishes Fries' philosophy from that of contemporary German philosophers who acknowledged intellectual intuition.[140]

2.2.2.1.2 THE CONCEPT OF TRUTH AND THE EXCLUSION OF THE THING IN ITSELF

However, Fries himself leaves some texts that suggest the exclusion of the thing in itself from his own philosophy. These texts set out his theory of truth. Fries, in reference to Kant, perceives two types of truth (*Wahrheit*). Truth in its common meaning is the accordance of a representation with its object; it is opposed to error, and Fries calls it transcendental truth.[141] In contrast, Fries gives another meaning of truth, the accordance of a mediate cognition with an immediate cognition; it is concerned with what we actually have in our minds,[142] and Fries names this empirical truth.[143] Based on this distinction, he explains that we are not capable of transcendental truth. If the accordance of a representation with its object verifies a truth, such an object must be the one beyond the representation, i.e., the thing in itself. However, Kant explains that the object of our cognition cannot be the object in itself.[144] Hence, we cannot compare representations in our minds with the object beyond the representation, i.e., the thing in itself.[145]

This rejection of transcendental truth accompanies the exclusion of the thing in itself. Fries notes that the rejection of transcendental truth means that it is not possible to tell without mediation how things in themselves are, but only how human reason knows and recognizes those things.[146] These texts suggest that Fries' philosophy may have no place to talk about the thing in itself.

Fries excludes the thing in itself from his philosophy in accordance with his theory of truth, although he leaves some texts that do acknowledge the role of the thing in itself in his philosophy. What do these contradictory portrayals mean, and how can this contradiction be resolved? To solve this problem, the following section reconsiders the argument in Fries' *Knowledge,*

Belief, and Aesthetic Sense, revealing the ambiguity of the thing in itself in his philosophy and his intentions.

2.2.2.2.2 The ambiguity of Fries' concept of the thing in itself

2.2.2.2.2.1 THE THING IN ITSELF IN RELATION TO TRANSCENDENTAL TRUTH

In *Knowledge, Belief, and Aesthetic Sense*, Fries explores the relation between the theory of truth and the thing in itself. He begins by formulating problems into a simple question: Does our knowledge refer to the thing in itself? He considers the validity of the concept of the thing in itself by treating this question in relation to the theory of truth.

Fries argues that if our knowledge refers to the thing in itself, this means that we are capable of transcendental truth. In this case, the objects of our experience must be the things in themselves, and they cannot be appearances distinguished from things in themselves. However, this is impossible, he notes, because objects of experience are not things in themselves.[147] Fries ultimately concludes that it is contradictory to acknowledge transcendental truth,[148] and that the object of our cognition is only appearance.

These arguments in *Knowledge, Belief, and Aesthetic Sense* suggest that here Fries regards the thing in itself as an object independent of appearance. From this viewpoint, he asks whether the object of experience is *either* appearance *or* the thing in itself. It is now evident that the thing in itself, excluded from the viewpoint of the theory of truth, is concerned here with the standpoint that regards objects of experience as things in themselves. In other words, such a standpoint implies the *confusion* of appearances and things in themselves.

According to Fries, acknowledgment of transcendental truth means an "arrogance of knowledge"[149] which dares to go beyond the limitations of human cognition. In this context, Fries criticizes the dogmatists who ignore the finitude of human cognition and acknowledge the possibility of intellectual intuition, i.e., German idealists. He takes Schelling's idea of indifference (*Indifferenz*) as an example, and notes that his theory can be formulated into a problem of transcendental truth.[150] On the basis of his own theory of truth, Fries attempts to show that intellectual intuition means the confusion of appearances and things in themselves, and that such confusion, and the concept of the thing in itself in this sense, inevitably imply contradictions.[151]

2.2.2.2.2.2 THE THING IN ITSELF AS AN ASPECT OF THINGS

In contrast, Fries offers another meaning of the concept of the thing in itself, after the exclusion of the thing in itself as depicted above. To define this concept, he carefully renames appearance, which becomes the "apparent way *of things*"[152] or "being *of things* in space and time,"[153] and the thing in itself, which becomes "an essence *of things*"[154] or "a being *of things* in themselves."[155]

In this case, the distinction between the appearance and the thing in itself does not mean a distinction between two objects independent from each other, but between two aspects of the same "thing." By including these aspects under the "thing" as a higher kind of concept, Fries tries to deconstruct the conventional meaning of the thing in itself, and to rebuild this concept to fit more appropriately into his philosophy.

In addition, according to Fries, the thing in itself in this sense can have a place in philosophy only by restricting the range of our knowledge, as the aspect of a thing that can be justified through this restriction alone and can never be known through our cognition. Through this definition of the thing in itself, Fries tries to make the concept into one that justly shows the finitude of human cognition, excluding the thing in itself as a result of epistemic arrogance.

2.2.2.3 Conclusion

This section has considered the meaning of the thing in itself in Fries' philosophy.

Fries' philosophy has been characterized in terms of his *acknowledgment* of the thing in itself. However, he himself *excludes* the thing in itself from his philosophy in accordance with his theory of truth.

To solve this problem, this section reconsidered the argument in *Knowledge, Belief, and Aesthetic Sense*. Fries uses his theory of truth in order to illuminate the faults in the conventional meaning of things in themselves. He does so by showing that a standpoint which acknowledges intellectual intuition and ignores the limitations of human knowledge, such as German idealism, results in the affirmation of the thing in itself, which is regarded as an object independent of appearances; this implies the *confusion* of the appearance and the thing in itself, leading to a contradiction.

In contrast, the new concept of the thing in itself in Fries' philosophy means an aspect of the thing, which he renames the essence of the thing. The thing in itself in this sense becomes possible only through the restriction of human knowledge.

Fries attempts, then, to illuminate the distinction between himself and the other German idealists by provocatively problematizing the concept of the thing in itself, using his theory of truth. He tries to convert the concept of the thing in itself into one more appropriate for his philosophy, and to establish his own philosophy as an alternative to German idealism.

It is now evident that Liebmann's critique of the concept of the thing in itself in Fries' philosophy was not valid, as Liebmann understood the concept of the thing in itself in the conventional sense, leading him to think that this concept is contradictory.[156] Fries' acknowledgment of the thing in itself does not mean its mere restoration, but its conversion.

Notes

1. Beiser [2014] offers a precise explanation of Fries' philosophy, and (albeit fragmentally) examines his philosophical method. Conversely, this book systematically examines Fries' *method of philosophy*, and reveals that its centralization and reconstruction are the key point of Fries' reception of Kant's critical philosophy.
2. In 1798, Fries commented that "while this [philosophical] viewpoint has been changed by Kant, the whole transcendental critique arises with the success of all Kantian philosophical works based on this viewpoint. Its success is no longer doubted now" (VePM, p. 157). In 1819: "What matters most is that I have contributed to describing a scientific system; that the clear Kantian investigation in the methodology is better recognized and more generally so regarding its product" (SL, p. IIX). And "hence, from a historical viewpoint my work follows Kant's great works and their decisively important investigations" (NaKV, I, p. XII).
3. SM, p. 90.
4. SPh, p. VI. Cf. SM, p. 89. According to Fries, because science, to which philosophy also belongs, is "no ingenious product of reason" (SPh, S. VI), "philosophy is a product of the independent self-activity of reason" (ibid.).
5. RFS, p. 245; SPh, p. 8; SM, p. 37.
6. Cf. Beiser [2014], p. 51.
7. NKV, I, p. XXI; NaKV, I, p. 15f.
8. Ibid.; NaKV, I, p. 16. Cf. NKV, I, p. 194; NaKV, I, p. 243; RFS, p. 219.
9. VePM, p. 176; RFS, p. 260.
10. SM, p. 91. Cf. NKV, I, p.14; NaKV, I, p. 9; Beiser [2014], p. 51.
11. NKV, II, p.14; NaKV, II, p. 9.
12. SM, p.118.
13. Ibid.
14. Beiser points out that in 1764 Fries could have read only the *Prolegomena* and the *Prize Essay*, and this determined the form his reception of Kant's philosophy took. Cf. Beiser [2014], p. 27.
15. However, the word "intuition" here means perception in the Kantian sense. Therefore, intuition here does not mean the immediate relation to the object that belongs only to one's sensibility as an isolated receptivity.
16. SPh, p. 56.
17. Ibid., p. 47.
18. Fries defines the term "consciousness" as follows: "Consciousness in the narrowest sense of the word means the inner self-cognition of cognitions, i.e., the cognition of the cognitions which we possess" (SPh, p. 54). In another place he defines it as "the inner cognition that such a cognition is lying in me" (ibid., p. 47). He also uses the word "re-consciousness" (*Wiederbewußtsein*) with respect to philosophical cognitions, in order to emphasize that they are brought

into consciousness only through the mediation of an analyzing operation (cf. Sph, pp. 47, 57; NKV, I, p. 94; NaKV, I, p. 136).
19 Cassirer [1920], p. 479.
Roberto [2007] also illuminates this aspect of Fries' concept of consciousness. Cf. Roberto [2007], p. 38.
20 Cf. SM, p. 40.
21 SM, p. 105.
22 SM, p. 100.
23 SM, p. 103.
24 Ibid.
25 Cf. RFS, p. 264.
26 SM, p. 102.
27 SM, p. 103.
28 SM, p. 110, NKV, I, S. 284; NaKV, I, S. 342.
29 SM, p. 104.
30 NKV, I, p. XXXVIII; NaKV, p. 31.
31 Because "speculation" aims to clarify the "cognition of reason," speculation as an art of philosophizing is distinguished from the "ordinary usage of understanding" (cf. NKV, I, p. 321; NaKV, I, p. 384). Roberto [2007] also examines the relationship between speculation and reflection. Cf. Roberto [2007], p. 40ff.
32 NKV, I, p. XXXIX; NaKV, I, p. 32.
33 SM, p. 105.
34 Gary Hatfield explains Fries' method as follows: "He did, in fact, call his theory of reason a 'physical' theory, but that meant only that he considered it to rest on inductive grounds, in the same manner as physics" (Hatfield [1990], p. 115). Hatfield refers here to NKV, II, p. 72 and I, pp. 25–26. However, as will be seen, Fries mentions that speculation as a philosophical method must be distinguished from induction, which can never ensure the apodicticity of cognition. Fries finds a similarity here between philosophy and physics, but only in the fact that philosophy also adopts the regressive or analytic method (NaKV, II, p. 26) on the basis of experience (NaKV, II, p. 72), which, however, does not mean that philosophy is essentially based on such induction.
35 NKV, I, p. 283; NaKV, I, p. 31; SM, p. 112.
36 Beiser characterizes deduction as follows: "[A] deduction attempts to show how it [a proposition] plays a necessary role within the general structure of our reason" (Beiser [2014], p. 75). The deduction, however, is defined according to (in Fries' words) the exhibition of the coincidence of judgment with our immediate cognition of reason. According to Fries, this deduction can be regarded as a kind of justification because it refers to the "immediate" cognition of reason. How, however, the deduction is possible is quite ambiguous in Fries' philosophy, as Beiser also explains. Cf. Beiser [2014], p. 76.
37 Cf. NKV, I, p. 281f.; NaKV, I, p. 339f.
38 NKV, I, p. 284; NaKV, I, p. 343.
39 Cf. KrV, B40.
40 Cf. KrV, B2f.
41 NKV, I, p. XXXVI; NaKV, I, p. 29.
42 NKV, I, p. XXXV; NaKV, I, p. 28. Cf. Bonnnet [2013], p. 37f.
43 Ibid.
44 NKV, I, p. XXXVII; NaKV, I, p. 29.
45 Ibid.

46 SM, p. 114.
47 NKV, I, p. XXXVI; NaKV, I, p. 29.
48 This chapter is based on Oota [2019], p. 92f.
49 Beiser [2014], pp. 11f., 24.
50 Fischer also says: "However, if these objects are not *a priori*, space and time are not intuitions *a priori*, categories are not concepts *a priori*, so I must ask: How does the critique of reason remain? As it is of Kantian spirit, it disappears, as well as its whole validity" (Fischer [1862], p. 18).
51 From this standpoint, he divided the German philosophers in Jena into two schools: The one to which Reinhold, Fichte, Schelling, and Hegel belonged, and the other, to which Fries belonged (cf. Fischer [1862], p. 7). Fischer called them the oldest and youngest Kantian schools (ibid.) and denied the latter's legitimacy, regarding the former as the proper development of Kantian philosophy. Cf. Bonnet [2013], p. 11f.
52 He regarded the philosophy of Fichte, Schelling, and Hegel as the idealist way (*Richtung*) (Liebmann [1865], p. 70), and Fries' philosophy as an empiricist way (ibid., p. 140).
53 Liebmann [1865], p. 150. Moreover, he appraises Fries' philosophy as follows: "Among those that can be made against the Kantian critique, it is the nastiest misunderstanding to regard it as a psychological one" (ibid.).
54 Windelband [1880], p. 386. Finally, he characterized Fries' philosophy, alongside Beneke's, with the word "psychologism."
55 This chapter is based on Oota [2019], p. 93f.
56 Cf. NKV, II, p. 11; NaKV, II, p. 8; SM, p. 114; VePM, p. 170. "Metaphysical cognition here means in general cognition *a priori* from concepts in synthetic judgments. Hence, metaphysics as a science made of them [concepts in synthetic judgments] must include a complete system of all synthetic judgments *a priori* made of concepts. […] However, all cognitions *a priori* must be apodictically certain [*apodiktisch gewiß*]" (VePM, p. 170).
57 Additionally, he claims: "Basically, philosophical cognition is either logical or transcendental or metaphysical, and always apodictic; assertoric, psychological cognition belongs only to elementary study [*Elementarlehre*] (critique), not to a philosophical system" (VePM, p. 183).
58 Nelson [1904], p. 43.
59 Ibid., p. 42f.
60 While Nelson's answer to Liebmann is also based on this distinction, it is invalid until this problem is solved.
61 This chapter is based on Oota [2019], p. 94.
62 Fries tends to use the word "apodictic" instead of "*a priori*" in his *New Critique of Reason*, even though such a distinction between the "assertoric" and the "apodictic" corresponds exactly to the Kantian distinction between the "*a posteriori*" and "*a priori*" (NKV, I, p. 249), because "such a distinction [between *a priori* and *a posteriori*] is […] often misleading" (NKV, I, p. 250); when the concept "a priori" is related to cognition, it could be mistaken for the innateness of cognition (ibid.), although all actual cognition is given to us through and with perception for the first time (ibid, p. 250f.), and it does not mean that the form on which such cognition is based arises from experience (ibid.). However, Fries also admits the apriority of such philosophical cognitions (Cf. SM, p. 80).
63 This chapter is based on Oota [2019], p. 95f.

64 VePM, p. 176; RFS, p. 58.
65 RFS, p. 260; VePM, p. 176.
66 VePM, p. 157f.; RFS, p. 301f.
67 SM, p. 91. Cf. NKV, II, p. 14; NaKV, II, pp. VI, 9.
68 SL, pp. 125, 159. Such real relations, whose representations reason contains as immediate cognitions, are also called "categories" (cf. SL, p. 159; GPh, II, p. 600f.).
69 NKV, II, p. 14; NaKV, II, p. VI, S. 9.
70 NaKV, II, p. VI.
71 NKV, I, p. 188; NaKV, p. 236; SL, p. 97f.
72 NKV, I, p. XXIII; NaKV, I, p. 17. Nelson also emphasizes that Fries' standpoint is distinct from both dogmatism and empiricism. He finds its grounding in Fries' idea of the immediate cognition of reason, as a source of cognition distinguished from mere sensibility and logical judgment (Nelson [1904], p. 55). However, such a presupposition of a new mental faculty may be justified for the first time as *the opinions* are identified as objects of analysis.
73 "Everyone adapts philosophical truths without difficulty, and in most cases unconsciously and unthinkingly. [...] If we then try to understand each other on the basis of those [philosophical truths], we find that our judgment in all those [philosophical] things starts from certain general presuppositions about [philosophical cognitions like] nature, moral living, and belief [...]" (SM, p. 89).
74 Bonsiepen [1997], p. 329.
75 NKV, I, p. 189; NaKV, I, p. 238.
76 Ibid.
77 NKV, I, p. 47; NaKV, I, p. 77.
78 SL, p. 93.
79 NKV, I, p. 47; NaKV, I, p. 77. From the fact that the cognitions of reason are presupposed through opinions, even if unconsciously, we are justified in regarding it as a presupposition of our opinions (Cf. NKV, II, p. 14; NaKV, II, p. 9). Concerning the actuality of synthetic cognition *a priori*, Fries takes the same standpoint as Kant. Nelson calls such a standpoint "the acknowledgment of the inevitable actuality of metaphysical presuppositions" (Nelson [1906], p. 57).
80 Beiser also emphasizes the important role of reflection in Fries' philosophy. Cf. Beiser [2014], p. 78. Bonnet also offers a precise explanation of the distinction between reason and understanding. Cf. Bonnet [2013], p. 187ff. However, Beiser and Bonnet do not focus on the role of "opinion" (*Beurteilung*) in Fries' philosophy.
81 SL, p. 159.
82 Ibid.
83 Ibid., p. 94.
84 Hasselblatt summarizes this relation between understanding and reason as follows: "Fries opposes understanding, the faculty of mediated cognition, to reason, the faculty of immediate cognition. The understanding brings forth cognition only based on the logical *form* of judgment regarding the content of this cognition the understanding must receive from reason" (Hasselblatt [1922], p. 29).
85 NKV, I, pp. 188f., 198ff.; NaKV, II, pp. 236f., 247ff.
86 NKV, I, p. 199f.; NaKV, II, p. 248f.

87 Ibid.
88 NKV, I, pp. 130f., 203; NaKV, I, pp. 175f., 253.
89 Beiser summarizes the role of reason as follows: "It is the spontaneous activity of reason itself that posits these laws, that creates this systematic structure, and that contains the immediate truths in terms of which all others are justified; but its activity is not immediately evident to consciousness, which rather presupposes its workings" (Beiser [2014], p. 77). Furthermore, Beiser finds a problem in Fries' standpoint: "How does the transcendental philosopher [i.e., a philosopher adopting Fries' standpoint] know that his reflection, his theory of reason, is an accurate account of the original activities of reason?" (Beiser [2014], p. 78). This problem is ultimately related to the possibility of "deduction" in Fries' philosophy. Fries does not offer a precise explanation of this problem, but rather attempts to ignore it by insisting that cognition of reason should be "immediate."
90 NKV, I, p. 190; NaKV, I, p. 239.
91 SL, p. 159.
92 NKV, I, p. 94; NaKV, I, p. 136, Cf. SPh, p. 78.
93 Bonnet also offers an explanation of this distinction. Cf. Bonnet [2013], p. 159ff.
94 NKV, I, p. 94; NaKV, I, p. 135. He owes this distinction to Ernst Plattner (cf. Plattner [1795], p. 40).
95 Ibid.
96 NKV, I, p. 159; NaKV, I, p. 205.
97 SM, p. 105.
98 Kant attributed both judgment and synthetic unity to understanding, which makes the table of judgment simultaneously the guidance for deducing the table of categories (cf. KrV, A66ff.=B91ff.; AAIV, p. 323f). To the contrary, Fries concedes no relationship between judgment and categories, and he attributes the categories to reason, while he attributes judgment to understanding (cf. Bonsiepen [1997], p. 330). Therefore, judgments provide information about neither categories nor the content of philosophy.
99 SL, p. 12.
100 This chapter is based on Oota [2019], p. 98f.
101 Nelson [1906], p. 23f.
102 Fries claims the same thing in his *System of Metaphysics*: "Every recognizing is an activity of our spirit [*Geist*]. Hence, all cognitions are objects of inner experience […]" (SM, p. 104).
103 He defines inner perception as cognition of cognitions in 1787 (VePM, p. 178). Afterwards, in the *System of Philosophy*, he defines it as follows: "[A] representation of which we are re-conscious is called 'perception' [*Perzeption*]" (SPh, p. 57). Additionally, "we […] can obtain [philosophical knowledge] only from inner consciousness of ourselves. The character of this inner perception is that it expresses itself in every particular case: 'I think,' 'I recognize,' 'I feel,' 'I desire,' 'I will'" (NKV, I, p. 6). "A clear representation is called 'perception' [*Perzeption*], in contrast to an obscure one" (NKV, I, p. 90) in the *New Critique of Reason*. "Perception is the consciousness of sensible intuitive cognitions" in the *System of Metaphysics* (SM, p. 29).
104 In this respect, Fries criticizes Kant: "Hence, his [Kant's] self-contradictory concept of 'transcendental faculties of mind' arose, which were not only supposed to be a source of cognitions *a priori*, but he also regarded their functions

as recognizable *a priori*, as if we had another source of self-cognition except inner experience" (SL, p. 32). Fries' standpoint rests on criticism that emphasizes the finitude of human cognitions on which the critique itself is also based.
105 Additionally, he carefully avoids the word "psychology" as he determines his method. "[Because any critique of reason concerns a human mind as an object of inner experience,] hence, it could be the science which is commonly called 'psychology,' but we avoid such a use of the word for certain reasons" (NKV, I, p. XLIII; NaKV, I, p. 36). "The original self-activity of reason in recognizing is the task [*Rätsel*] of psychology in the ordinary sense, but in fact it is not our topic" (NKV, I, p. 310; NaKV, I, p. 372). Cf. Leary [1982], p. 231ff.
106 An example can be found in his distinction between mental faculties: "[…T]he better theory of consciousness, and distinction between the self-activity (spontaneity) of reason and arbitrariness of thinking understanding, is already known more generally" (SM, p. 73). This definition of mental faculties plays a vital role in Fries' philosophy, as we have seen.
107 VePM, p. 165.
108 Ibid.
109 Ibid.
110 VePM, p. 164f.
111 VePM, p. 176.
112 VePM, p. 164f.
113 SM, p. 99.
114 SM, p. 89.
115 Cf. NKV, II, p. 14; SM, p. 91.
116 Cf. NKV, I, p. 188.
117 NKV, I, p. 233.
118 NKV, I, p. 234.
119 RFS, p. 236.
120 NKV, I, p. 234.
121 RFS, p. 236.
122 NKV, I, p. 233.
123 NKV, I, p. 252.
124 NKV, I, p. 253.
125 Ibid.
126 NKV, I, p. 253.
127 NKV, I, p. 260.
128 Bonnet also offers an explanation of the feeling of truth (Bonnet [2013], p. 129ff.). However, Bonnet's analysis of this concept is based on the description in the *New or Anthropological Critique of Reason*. In contrast, this chapter examines the developmental history of this concept, in order to clarify the development of Fries' philosophical views themselves in accordance with the changing roles played by the "feeling of truth."
129 In the *New or Anthropological Critique of Reason* (1829–1831), which is the revised version of the *New Critique of Reason*, the descriptions cited above are revised, and Fries provides more precise explanations of the concept of the feeling of truth (cf. NaKV, I, p. 405f).
130 Cf. Ibid.
131 Fries refers to this concept twice in the *New Critique of Reason*. In addition to the description cited above, he refers to the feeling of truth, aesthetic

feeling (*ästhetisches Gefühl*) and moral feeling, and criticizes them in relation to English thought (*englische Untersuchung*), stating that the English thinker confuses these kinds of feelings with mere sensation (NKV, I, p. 75).
132 Cf. NKV, II, p. 11; NaKV, II, p. 8; SM, p. 114; VePM, p. 170. "Metaphysical cognition here means in general cognition *a priori* from concepts in synthetic judgments. Hence, metaphysics as a science made of them [concepts in synthetic judgments] must include a complete system of all synthetic judgments *a priori* made of concepts. / [...] However, all cognitions *a priori* must be apodictically certain [*apodiktisch gewiß*]" (VePM, p. 170).
133 Additionally, he claims: "Basically, philosophical cognition is either logical or transcendental or metaphysical, and always apodictic; assertoric, psychological cognition belongs only to elementary study [*Elementarlehre*] (critique), not to the system of philosophy" (VePM, p. 183).
134 VePM, p. 176; RFS, p. 58.
135 RFS, p. 260; VePM, p. 176.
136 VePM, p. 157f.; RFS, p. 301f.
137 These sentences are similar to the description given in NKV, I, p. 342. However, compared with the description of the feeling of truth in *Reinhold, Fichte, and Schelling*, Fries refines this sentence in the *New Critique of Reason* to explain his developed conceptions of this concept more precisely.
138 Cf. SM, p. 73.
139 Beiser [2014], p. 154.
140 Liebmann [1865], p. 79.
141 NKV, I, p. 287; WGA, p. 29.
142 NKV, I, p. 340.
143 Ibid.
144 NKV, II, p. 180.
145 NKV, II, p. 179f.
146 NKV, I p. 295.
147 WGA, p. 48.
148 Cf. Beiser [2014], p. 75.
149 WGA, p. 60.
150 Cf. NKV, II, p. 178.
151 GWA, p. 47.
152 NKV, II, p. 5; WGA, p. 108.
153 Cf. WGA, p. 128.
154 Cf. NKV, II, p. 157.
155 Ibid.; WGA, pp. 52, 58.
156 Liebmann [1865], p. 156.

3 The Friesian and Neo-Friesian schools

3.1 The Friesian school

This chapter examines the philosophical development of the Friesian school.

It is often believed that the philosophy of nature in 19th-century German philosophy, especially in German idealism, is speculative to the point of anachronism and was minimally influential on the development of the natural sciences. A forgotten philosophical movement in 19th-century Germany, however, had a significant influence on the natural sciences at the time.

This forgotten movement was the Friesian school, a philosophical stream of thought based on the philosophy of Jakob Friedrich Fries. After Fries' death, his disciple, Ernst Friedrich Apelt (1812–1859), founded the Friesian school. Following Fries' philosophy, which thematized the method of philosophy and radicalized Kantian criticism from an empiricist standpoint, Apelt attempted to bridge the gap between philosophy and the natural sciences of his period by focusing on induction as a method of natural science.

In *The Theory of Induction* (*Die Theorie der Induction*), Apelt thematizes induction as a scientific method and investigates it from the standpoint of Friesian philosophy. He finds its justification in the precise distinction between induction and abstraction, and claims that, while abstraction provides cognition of higher principles, induction verifies their validity through experience. Apelt's philosophy, developed from Fries' theories, influenced the contemporary natural sciences. For example, Matthias Jacob Schleiden, a member of the Friesian school and a well-known botanist, in his *Elements of Scientific Botany* (*Grundzüge der Wissenschaftlichen Botanik*) also thematizes the roles of induction and abstraction, and bases his methodology on Apelt's philosophy in advance of his investigation of natural science.

First, this chapter examines Apelt's ideas. In his *Theory of Induction*, Apelt focuses on the role of induction following Fries' philosophical approach. Apelt emphasizes, on the one hand, the role of experience, and on the other, in his *Metaphysics*, the role of that immediate cognition of reason which justifies philosophical cognition gained through abstraction. Next, the chapter examines Matthias Jacob Schleiden's methodology. Schleiden's emphasis on induction in relation to investigations by the natural sciences is based on Apelt's interpretation of Fries' ideas, i.e., his emphasis on induction and on the distinction between induction and abstraction.

3.1.1 The rise of the Friesian school

Fries' philosophy, as presented in the previous section, repeatedly appeared through the establishment of two Friesian schools. Ernst Friedrich Apelt (1812–1859) established the first Friesian school (*Fries'sche Schule*) by publishing *Papers of the Friesian School* (*Abhandlungen der Fries'schen Schule*) in 1847. This is the first series of the Friesian school's journal.[1]

The first Friesian school had a significant influence on German natural scientists of that period,[2] initiated through the publication of *Abhandlungen der Fries'schen Schule*. The preface of the first volume declared that the editors of this volume came together to publish papers that, in spite of the differences of character and [academic] rank among the authors, were accomplished in the same spirit, i.e., the spirit of the critical school that Kant established and Fries further cultivated.[3] As discussed above, the Friesian school characterized the philosophical stream of thought from Fries to Kant as critical philosophy, and criticized the natural philosophy of Fichte, Hegel, and Schelling for distancing itself from the actual natural sciences.[4] From this perspective, the first Friesian school problematized the relationship of philosophy and the natural sciences,[5] and published its journals from this standpoint.

Simultaneously, Apelt, a proponent of the first Friesian school, contributed to its activity by publishing many books addressing transdisciplinary areas from the perspective of Friesian philosophy, and by publishing the journal of the Friesian school. Apelt's reception of Friesian philosophy can be characterized by an emphasis on the immediate cognition of reason[6] and the centralization of the role of induction (*Induktion*) in building a bridge between philosophy and natural science.[7] The activity of the first Friesian school ended with Apelt's death only ten years after the journal's publication.

Apelt was born in Bogatynia in 1812, and became interested in astronomy during his gymnasium years in Zittau. He entered Jena University in 1831, studied philosophy and mathematics under Fries, and briefly studied the natural sciences, including astronomy, at Leipzig; here Apelt came into contact with Hermann Lotze, who introduced him to Fries' own philosophy.[8] After being promoted at Jena University in 1835, Apelt obtained his habilitation in 1839 and taught mathematics, natural science, and then philosophy. He was promoted to extraordinary professor (*außerordentlicher Professor*) in 1840, and full professor in 1856.⁹

3.1.2 Ernst Friedrich Apelt's views

While Apelt's activity spanned many areas, from the natural sciences to religious studies, his thought has primarily influenced the natural sciences and metaphysics. His reception of Fries' philosophy includes two characteristics: on the one hand, Apelt attempts to combine Fries' philosophy with the natural sciences by focusing on the role of induction, while on the other hand, he tries to refine Fries' metaphysics by emphasizing the role of the immediate cognition of reason in Fries' philosophy. The following section offers an overview of how Fries' philosophy influenced Apelt's.

3.1.2.1 Apelt's standpoint in The Theory of Induction and its influence

3.1.2.1.1 EMPHASIS ON INDUCTION IN *THE THEORY OF INDUCTION*

The Theory of Induction (1854), one of Apelt's most important philosophical works, promoted a common interpretation involving a characterization of Fries' standpoint in relation to its emphasis on induction.[10] In this book, Apelt thematizes the relationship between philosophy and natural science, and between British and German philosophy. He finds induction to be the intersection between them and attempts to re-examine the concept of induction from a Friesian perspective by claiming that it has been misunderstood in both English and German philosophy.

> A double interest is combined with induction: it builds bridges between philosophy and the natural sciences on the one hand; it is a central difference between German and English philosophy on the other hand. Although the philosophy dominating Germany now refuses or overlooks induction, since Bacon, English and French philosophers have made an effort to ground and formulate philosophy in the way of induction. Here, harmony and equilibrium might be possible only through the appropriate theory of induction. The reason that divides the manners of German and English philosophical thinking has also torn the bond between philosophy and natural science in our [German] case. Since Kepler and Newton, natural science has made significant developments through induction. Conversely, Leibniz has prescribed the way of rationalistic speculation for German philosophy, and the power that his genius exercised on the spirit of the German people and the

way of their philosophical thinking could not be broken even by Kant's critique of reason.

(Apelt [1854], p. V)

Emphasizing the role of induction in science, then, Apelt criticizes the "rationalistic speculation" represented by Leibniz and attempts to defend the role of experience in philosophizing. Simultaneously, in accordance with Fries' perspective, Apelt emphasizes the distinction between induction and abstraction to distinguish his own standpoint from pre-Kantian empiricism.

On the one hand, Fries emphasizes the role of experience in philosophizing, from the standpoint of ordinary opinions in daily life, by adopting the regressive method and claiming that both abstraction and induction belong to it.[11] On the other hand, Fries also focuses on the distinction between induction and abstraction[12] by arguing that abstraction, the essence of philosophical speculation, has been generally misunderstood because speculation has been confused with induction.[13] Fries locates the characteristics of philosophical abstraction in the fact that we become conscious of general necessary truths not through induction but through abstraction;[14] he summarizes the distinction between abstraction and induction as follows:

> Speculation, which exhibits the general principle standing beyond given particulars through abstraction and analysis. And induction, which verifies the general principle of speculation from particulars through combination and comparison.
>
> (NKV, I, p. 321; NaKV, I, p. 383)[15]

Apelt also adheres to Fries' distinction between induction and abstraction. In a chapter entitled "Induction and Abstraction" in *The Theory of Induction*, Apelt claims that principles must be recognized through abstraction before induction is used as a method of verification.

> *Induction is not the way to necessary truths, but the way to connect necessary truth with accidental truths.* Induction is a bond that firmly combines the possible and necessary with the actual. Therefore it must be a way other than the way of induction that leads to the necessary ground truths, and this is the way of *abstraction*.
>
> (Apelt [1854], p. 56)

Abstraction as well as induction are regressive ways of thinking, i.e., a retrogression from the particular to the general. However, the fashion of regression from the particular to the general is completely different in this way and in that. Induction regresses through verification, abstraction through *analysis*. [...] Induction verifies the validity of a principle from many cases; abstraction exhibits the validity of a principle in a single example. Induction lets us recognize which principle follows from the relations of certain facts; abstraction lets us recognize which principle is already presupposed by a certain claim. While knowledge of all or at least many cases belongs to induction, just a single case is enough for abstraction.

(Apelt [1854], p. 56f)

From this perspective, Apelt attributes the mental faculty of abstraction to that of "understanding" (*Verstand*).[16]

While Apelt also refers to the distinction between induction and abstraction, he does not examine the concepts of "deduction" and "immediate cognition of reason," which Fries thematizes as key concepts in his philosophy.[17] Moreover, while Apelt emphasizes the role of abstraction in investigating philosophical principles,[18] he identifies the criterion for justifying the principles abstraction discovers with the completeness of the scientific system that these principles constitute. Apelt calls this scientific system "theory" and explains this as follows:

Theory in the narrowest sense of this word signifies a science in which facts are recognized in their subordination under the necessary principle and their coherence is explained by these principles. [...] No matter whether the science consists of homogeneous or heterogeneous cognitions, in the case of all science logic requires the systematic unity of all propositions of that science, i.e., the complete subordination of the particular [*das Besondere*] under the general principle [*das Allgemeine*].

(Apelt [1854], p. 65)

Here Apelt finds the conditions for forming propositions as components of a science, in that these propositions constitute a system[19] through subordination to higher principles. In order to emphasize the role of systematicity in the sciences, Apelt then establishes the "scientific architectonic"[20] as a discipline concerning the formation of scientific systems.

3.1.2.1.2 POPPER'S RECEPTION OF FRIES' PHILOSOPHY THROUGH APELT'S *THEORY OF INDUCTION*

Apelt's use of Fries' philosophy in his *Theory of Induction* had a significant influence on interpretations of Fries' thought in the 20th century. The following section examines one example: Karl Popper's interpretation of Fries' philosophy.

Popper often refers to and criticizes Fries' philosophy, such as in his famous conception of the Friesian Trilemma[21] in *The Logic of Scientific Discovery* (1959) (the English version of Popper's *Logik der Forschung*, originally published in German in 1935). Popper confronts Fries' philosophy in *The Two Fundamental Problems of the Theory of Knowledge* (1979).[22] This manuscript includes notes Popper made between 1930 and 1933 examining central ideas for *The Logic of Scientific Discovery*. In the manuscript, Popper attempts to grasp Fries' concept of the immediate cognition of reason and his theory of reason in relation to Fries' concept of induction.

> The existence of *a priori*, that is, universally valid and necessary, "immediate knowledge" can thus be demonstrated only through universal psychological statements, or through psychological principles; Fries therefore speaks of an (empirical-psychological) "theory of reason," from which the existence of "immediate knowledge" of *a priori* statements is said to be deducible. [...] This "theory of reason," however, can only be obtained by induction. The Friesian critical-empirical method is distinguished from the dogmatic methods of a "one-sided rationalism" and of a "one-sided empiricism" precisely by the fact that "in the struggle against these two ... it has been forced ... to derive the highest principles of our theory of transcendental apperception by inductions from our internal experience." [...] The theory of reason thus presupposes the admissibility of induction, and presupposes that universal empirical statements can be formulated and verified in an inductive fashion. [...] According to Fries' apriorist premises, the inductive procedure is admissible only if an *a priori* principle of induction is valid.
>
> (Popper [1979], p. 113f.; English translation, p. 255f., partially modified by the author)

At the end of the above quotation, Popper notes Apelt's *Theory of Induction* as a source of Fries' apriorist premise. Although the kind of interpretation of Fries' philosophy that Popper performs here echoes that of Leonard Nelson, a founder of the Neo-Friesian school who had a significant influence on the formation of Popper's thought, it is to Apelt's *Theory of Induction* that Popper refers in justifying his interpretation of Fries' philosophy. As shown above, Apelt's interpretation of Fries' philosophy, as described in his *Theory of Induction*, had a significant influence on how Fries' philosophy has been interpreted for posterity.

3.1.2.2 Apelt's views in his Metaphysics

3.1.2.2.1 EMPHASIS ON IMMEDIATE COGNITION OF REASON IN APELT'S METAPHYSICS

Three years after the publication of *The Theory of Induction*, Apelt published his most significant book, *Metaphysics* (1857). While Apelt praises Fries' *System of Metaphysics*,[23] in the beginning of his own book Apelt also indicates its excessively dogmatic form of description[24] as a problem upon which he intends to improve.

In contrast to *The System of Induction*, Apelt's *Metaphysics* emphasizes the role of the "immediate cognition of reason." Apelt attempts to defend Fries' view of philosophy's method by characterizing what Fries called the "standpoint of ordinary opinions in daily life" as an "actuality [*Wirklichkeit*] of philosophical cognition *a priori*."[25] Apelt claims:

> These objects of [mathematical and geometrical] cognition are actually given through the intuition. However, it cannot be determined through intuition whether what is claimed in metaphysical judgment is also in fact so. Therefore, if the truth of such philosophical cognitions *a priori* could not be indicated in at least one case *in concreto*, i.e., if the actuality of these philosophical cognitions could not be indicated, it would be also doubtful whether what we say is concerned with objects of actuality or only objects of delusion [*Einbildungskraft*]. Such a case is given, in fact. As we will see, we can explain the reality and actuality of metaphysical cognition not through *construction*, like that of mathematics indeed, but wholly through *factum*.
> (Apelt [1857], p. 56f.)

As shown above, Apelt emphasizes the nature of the philosophical cognitions *a priori* constructing our metaphysical judgments: They are actually given in a manner different from mathematical or geometrical cognitions, which are given through the intuition.

From this perspective, Apelt emphasizes the role of the immediate cognition of reason as the "third thing" (*das Dritte*)[26] that enables philosophical cognition *a priori* or synthetic judgment *a priori*, which can be reduced to neither logical form nor mathematical construction through intuition.

> Through this [transcendental guidance], metaphysics achieves its fixed base of its cognitions just as geometry possesses one in the intuition of space. Except for space and time, there is also a third thing, an analogue of them, which is not immediately clear but can be made clear only mediately and artificially – it is a obscure space, so to speak, and this

third thing is a seat and source of metaphysical truths just as well as the space is a seat and source of geometrical truths.
(Apelt [1857], p. VII)

The understanding (faculty of thinking) is only a faculty of reflection, i.e., only a faculty of repetition or higher consciousness of immediate cognitions. Therefore, reflection can provide itself only with analytic judgments and the consequences of the inferences made from them. However, [insomuch as all judgments are described in the form of judgments] all synthetic judgments include a mediate cognition that another immediate cognition must underlie. Such an immediate cognition is an intuition of the senses for empirical judgments and an intuition of space for geometrical judgments. Accordingly, there must also be such an immediate cognition behind metaphysical judgments. Without this background of cognition that remains constant, we would not be able to recognize necessary truths through mere thinking, i.e., an arbitrary fashion of representation. Without such a source that lies behind the understanding, there could not be synthetic judgments from mere concepts, because no synthetic judgments, only analytic ones, can be derived from the understanding under its original emptiness.
(Apelt [1857], p. 94f.)

As this shows, Apelt follows Fries' distinction between understanding, as a faculty of reflection, and reason, which contains "immediate cognitions." Apelt attempts to defend Fries' perspective by emphasizing the reality or actuality of metaphysical cognition and connects that reality to the immediate cognition of reason. This aspect of Apelt's argument was also defended by Leonard Nelson.

In addition to referring to the actuality of synthetic judgments *a priori,* Apelt focuses on the homogeneity (*Gleichartigkeit*)[27] of metaphysical cognition with mathematical and geometrical cognition. He defends the actual existence of metaphysical cognition by comparing it with mathematical and geometrical cognitions, which are given through intuitions. As such, Apelt emphasizes the objective validity of metaphysical cognition.[28]

There is complete homogeneity between intuition and immediate cognition of pure reason, which we express in judgments. Accordingly, objective validity is also given to philosophical cognition. The principle (the form of necessity) exists only for consciousness when recognizing particular actual things; in *immediate cognition* it is already immediately combined with the latter.
(Apelt [1857], p. 535)

Wolfgang Röd considers Apelt's interpretation of Fries' philosophy to be characterized by its emphasis on the immediate cognition of reason.[29] In fact, Apelt focuses on the actuality of metaphysical cognition and thereby considers metaphysical cognition to be homogeneous with mathematical cognition; this leads to the autonomy of the immediate cognition of reason. Accordingly, the role of philosophy is restricted to the repetition of the immediate cognition of reason in consciousness, i.e., the "re-consciousness" (*Wiederbewusstsein*)[30] of it.[31]

As addressed above, in *Metaphysics*, Apelt illuminates the role of the immediate cognition of reason by appealing to the actuality of synthetic judgment *a priori* on the one hand and, on the other hand, emphasizes the objective validity of the immediate cognition of reason by asserting its homogeneity with intuition, i.e., with mathematical or geometrical cognition. In this sense, Apelt's interpretation of Fries' philosophy in *Metaphysics* emphasizes continuity between philosophical cognition and cognition in the natural sciences.

3.1.2.2.2 CASSIRER'S INTERPRETATION OF FRIES' PHILOSOPHY THROUGH APELT'S *METAPHYSICS*

Apelt's reception of Fries' philosophy had a significant influence on its later interpretation, which included many critiques of it. For example, Ernst Cassirer, a Neo-Kantian philosopher of the Marburg school, criticizes Fries' philosophy in *The Problem of Knowledge* (*Erkenntnisproblem*) by invoking Apelt's description of it.

Cassirer refers to Apelt's *Metaphysics*, supporting Apelt's standpoint and emphasizing the role of the immediate cognition of reason. He identifies the aim of Fries' philosophy with mere re-consciousness of this immediate cognition. Cassirer criticizes Fries' thought by claiming that "the reason itself becomes, [...] strictly speaking, a mere *thing* that is strange and opposed to the reason, like other things"[32] in Fries' philosophy. Cassirer also claims that "the presupposition of the superempirical [immediate cognition of reason], which is not a principle but a thing, necessarily makes Fries a psychological dogmatist."[33] As such, Cassirer criticizes Fries' thought as a form of psychologism by invoking Apelt's interpretation in order to emphasize the role of the immediate cognition of reason.[34]

3.1.3 Matthias Jacob Schleiden's methodological perspective

3.1.3.1 Schleiden's emphasis on Fries' philosophy

Fries' philosophy and Apelt's interpretation of it significantly influenced natural science. This chapter examines Matthias Jacob Schleiden's reference to Fries' thought and its similarity to Apelt's interpretation.

Schleiden was a botanist well known for his famous cell theory (*Zelltheorie*), a doctrine proposing that living organisms are made of cells. He was also known as a member of the Friesian school. He participated in producing *Papers of the Friesian School* (*Abhandlungen der Fries'schen Schule*) with Apelt, and wrote a short philosophical paper that criticizes Schelling and Hegel's natural philosophy for its distance from actual natural science, approving of Fries' philosophy from this viewpoint.

Schleiden's emphasis on Fries' position is also found in his works on botany. For example, in his *Elements of Scientific Botany with a Methodological Introduction* (*Grundzüge der Wissenschaftlichen Botanik nebst einer Methodologischen Einleitung*) he illuminates the importance of Fries' theories of philosophical methodology for contemporary science and for his own investigation of botany:

> The first is [...] the relation of this discipline [botany] to philosophy. [...T]he great developments that occur from the discovery of America to *Newton* wholly belong to the natural sciences. [...] Conversely, natural science has to own to philosophy at first, and recent definite progress depends on the general concession to wholesome Kantian–Friesian philosophy.
>
> (Schleiden [1861], p. 5)

> Botany is a branch of one and all natural science. Therefore, botany already presupposes a part of the (more general) natural sciences: physics and chemistry. Accordingly, physics and chemistry appear as indispensable background knowledge. Second, botany is, however, also a science; therefore it is a product of the activity of human cognition in the highest degree. However, this activity can err, and strays by being misled. If we want to find the truth, we must know the principle according to which the cognitive power should work. Botany presupposes philosophical cultivation, i.e., the knowledge of a theory of cognizant reason based on empirical psychology; in one word, critical or Kantian–Friesian philosophy.
>
> (Schleiden [1846], p. 1)

Here Schleiden claims that the botany "is a product of the activity of human cognition in the highest degree" and therefore requires investigation through human cognition, i.e., "critical or Kantian–Friesian philosophy" as the basis for the investigation of botany.

3.1.3.2 The relationship between Apelt and Schleiden

The relationship between Fries' philosophy and Schleiden's methodological views has been discussed by researchers.[35] One of the most significant examples is Cassirer's analysis of Schleiden's methodological standpoint in *The Problem of Knowledge* (*Erkenntnisproblem*). Regarding the relationship between Schleiden and Friesian thought, however, Cassirer merely refers to the role induction plays in Schleiden's views about botanical methodology. Cassirer focuses instead on the problem of developmental history[36] in relation to the history of natural science from Goethe to Darwin.

Despite this attention from researchers, including Cassirer, they have hitherto overlooked Apelt's influence on Schleiden's interpretation of Fries' philosophy. Although Schleiden himself does not often mention Apelt's name, his emphasis on induction as a method of natural science is based on Apelt's interpretation of this concept. Schleiden's emphasis on induction presupposes the distinction between induction and abstraction; and, further, the concept of induction here presupposes the process of abstraction that should be performed prior to induction. This chapter next examines Schleiden's position regarding induction and abstraction.

3.1.3.3 Schleiden's distinction between induction and abstraction

Schleiden's examination of the role of abstraction begins with a critique of Schelling and Hegel's *dogmatic* approach to natural philosophy. Schleiden finds the cause of this dogmatism in their defective use of abstraction:

> In this case [of investigation on organisms], empirical impossibility hides behind uncertain and defective abstraction [...]. In this case, some words, like organism, life, compulsion, soul, etc. are just the disguise of ignorance or unclarity, and wholesome [*gesund*] philosophical cultivation can only claim: "This is the correct way of abstraction; hereby we are brought to these certain distinctions with which we combine this very certain word as a sign." However, philosophers straying into a dogmatic approach, especially the Schellingian and Hegelian school under recent philosophers, escape from such a mode [...].
> (Schleiden [1861], p. 5f.)

Schleiden, then, finds the point of "wholesome philosophical cultivation" in "the correct way of abstraction," in contrast with the Schellingian and Hegelian schools' defective abstraction. Schleiden claims that such a deficiency in the Schellingian and Hegelian schools' abstraction is symbolized by the concept of an "organism" which is thematized in their schools. Thus, Schleiden opposes Fries' view to the dogmatic approach. He identifies the method of natural science with induction, and attempts to refine the role of abstraction in relation to the role of induction.

We, the followers of Fries, oppose these dogmatizing and systematizing methods to the inductive and heuristic method as the only justified method. In pure philosophy, we call this method a critical method because of its characteristics. The task of this critical method is the development of a theory of reason, and the deduction of all immediate cognition derived from that reason. Its tool, of course, is self-observation with a sharp analysis of concepts by forming the method of abstraction corresponding to their nature; however, in the applied philosophical disciplines and in the natural sciences we call this method an inductive method in a narrower sense. The characteristics of this method lie in the following: We ignore all hypotheses at first; presuppose no principle; immediately depart from certain things, particular facts; attempt to extract these things purely and completely; order them according to their inner relationship. Then we examine the principle under which these things occur and which they presuppose as a condition of their existence, and we advance regressively until we arrive at the highest concepts and principles, in which further derivations are evidently impossible.

(Schleiden [1861], p. 17)

Here Schleiden examines the role of abstraction in relation to induction. Following Fries' (and Apelt's) standpoint, Schleiden claims that the task of philosophy is "the development of a theory of reason, and the deduction of all immediate cognition derived from that reason." He locates its method in self-observation, in Fries' sense, and in "analysis of concepts." Accordingly, he calls all processes of investigation, including both abstraction and inductive verification, "the inductive method." In this sense, Schleiden's notion of the inductive method includes the process of abstraction.

Based on this methodological insight, Schleiden examines the case of the discovery of the principles of the cell through the analogy of a cell and a crystal, as an example of the proper use of abstraction and induction. Referring to Theodor Schwann, who was also known as a proponent of cell theory, Schleiden continues:

> Therefore, even if particular cells reproduce vegetatively and pass through all possible stages of cell life, and even if they are generally determined as a vegetative form, in addition to other simple plants, the particular cells themselves, not as a certain species, can be assumed [to be real]. Moreover, even if we do not agree with Schwann's parallelism between a cell and a crystal, and explain it as totally incomplete, in this spirited exposition the undeniable possibility is always suggested that natural science can grasp the cell as a necessary form of a relatively fixed

state of a permeable (assimilated, organic) material, just as the crystal can be grasped as impermeable (inorganic) material. However, in this case, all organisms occurring and vegetatively reproducing would be a certain species of organic crystallization, and there might have been great progress from these crystallizations to definite plant species, i.e., to the connection of these organic crystal forms with a specific, certain shape; and this great progress might justify our inserting this as a proper class between crystals, on the one hand, and plants and animals on the other.

(Schleiden [1861], p. 635)

Here Schleiden claims that a common property can be found in the formation of cells and in crystallization, based on the principle of morphology. Addressing the question of how the investigation of such a property is possible, he focuses on the scientific methodology that enables us to find the common property which the nature of cells and crystallization share, and finds its source in "a subjective source" of our spirit. Schleiden finds the basis of such an investigation in the *formation of concept* in our spirit, i.e., the way of abstraction.

If we also inquire into the characteristic property of the concept "species" in organic beings, only the following consideration can guide us. The principle of specification originates by nature from a subjective source; the reason why we must fix species and genera as objects of our spiritual activity lies in our way, and fashions how our concepts and abstractions are formed [...]. However, because of this subjective source, if nature corresponds to us and provides objective validity to the subjective way of grasping through experience, the principle of specification for our scientific cognition of nature remains meaningless. [...A]lthough we understand less sharply because of its more complicated relationship to time, we find the principle of specification clearly apparent in crystals. In this case, we owe to mathematics its sharp determination. However, in the case of organisms, our power of grasping abandons us, and only very precise inductions enable us to validate the principle in this case also.

(Schleiden [1861], pp. 635–636)

As shown above, abstraction is expected to provide cognition of the general principle that is supposed to regulate both the appearances of crystals and those of plants. After this process of abstraction, the discovered principle must be verified through induction to confirm its objective validity. In this sense, Schleiden's concept of induction follows Apelt's views regarding induction and abstraction.

3.1.4 Conclusion

This section has examined Apelt's ideas. In his *Theory of Induction*, he emphasizes the role of induction following Fries' philosophical standpoint. On the one hand, Apelt emphasizes the role of experience, and on the other, in his *Metaphysics*, the role of that immediate cognition of reason which justifies the philosophical cognition gained through abstraction.

This section also explored Schleiden's methodological views. He emphasizes the significance of Fries' philosophy in the investigations of the natural sciences, and the role of induction as a scientific method. Schleiden's discussion is based on Apelt's interpretation of the methods of Fries' philosophy. This interpretation emphasizes induction, and the distinction between induction and abstraction.

As explained above, Schleiden's emphasis on induction as a scientific method is based on the interpretation of Fries' philosophical method which was formulated by Apelt, the philosopher who founded and headed the first Friesian school.

3.2 The Neo-Friesian school

3.2.1 Nelson and the rise of the Neo-Friesian school

After the end of the Friesian school's activities, Fries' philosophy regained prominence with the rise of the Neo-Friesian school (*Neufries'sche Schule*), which was established in 1903 as a small academic group.[37] Leonard Nelson (1882–1927), a founder of the Neo-Friesian school, began to publish the *Papers of Fries' School: New Series* (*Abhandlungen der Fries'schen Schule: Neue Folge*) in 1904.[38] In response to contemporary thinkers' interest in Fries' philosophy,[39] Nelson established the Jakob Friedrich Fries Association (*Jakob Friedrich Fries-Gesellschaft*) in 1913,[40] and held conferences in 1914 and 1921.[41] The activity of the Neo-Friesian school was based on Nelson's efforts in Göttingen.[42]

Nelson devoted his life to reevaluating Fries' philosophy,[43] and developed his own thought from Fries' philosophical groundwork. Nelson's activity can similarly be characterized by antagonism against the so-called Neo-Kantian movement. Nelson's thought and the activity of the Neo-Friesian school had a significant influence on many fields, such as mathematics, natural science, logic, pedagogy, and political thought. The formation of Nelson's thought, however, began with his reception of Fries' philosophy, which continued to shape the entirety of Nelson's philosophy.

3.2.2 Nelson's reception of Fries' philosophy

3.2.2.1 Nelson's reception of Fries' philosophy: Contra the critics of Fries

Nelson's reception of Fries' philosophy began with his opposition to the critique of Fries' philosophy by Neo-Hegelian thinkers like Kuno Fischer. Nelson's dissertation aims to respond to Fischer, Max Scheler, and Theodor Elsenhans' characterization of Fries' philosophy as psychologism. In it, Nelson claims that "Fries was never a psychologist but rather fought against the psychologism of his contemporaries most drastically, and investigated the true salvation for philosophy's progression [*Fortbildung*] in liberation from psychologism."[44] As an example of Fries' fight against psychologism, Nelson cites Fries' critique of Reinhold, Fichte, and Schelling. Fries criticizes them by pointing out that they adopt a progressive, or synthetic, method that starts from a first principle. He claims that Reinhold, Fichte, and Schelling regard the products of self-observation of an inner experience as a metaphysical first principle and, therefore, confuse psychological cognition with that first principle. According to Nelson, Fries' critique of the German idealists shows his attempt to avoid confusion between psychological and philosophical cognition,[45] and to distinguish between them.

In addition, Nelson emphasizes the different meanings of the concept of "psychology" in Kant's and Fries' periods. Nelson claims that Kant attempted to distinguish transcendental philosophy from psychology only because "in Kant's period psychology was surely restricted to the field of a purely descriptive and genetic way of inquiry."[46] On the contrary, Fries defines psychology as a "science of inner experience."[47] Nelson concludes that Fries' emphasis on the role of psychology in philosophy does not indicate confusion between philosophy and psychology.[48]

3.2.2.2 Nelson's interpretation of Fries' philosophy: The problem of justifying philosophical cognition

As described above, in his dissertation, Nelson offers a reinterpretation of Fries' thought. Nelson begins this reconstruction of Fries' thought by emphasizing the role of the regressive method in philosophy:

> Therefore, when we take the kinds of judgments [*Urteile*] and opinions [*Beurteilungen*] [that constitute our daily philosophical convictions] from experiences of life, we can analyze them and inquire through the regressive method into the philosophical principles which are applied [*Anwendung kommen*] in our present judgments and opinions, and are commonly presupposed. Through the progressive analysis and

abstraction of particular examples [*die besonderen Anwendungen*] we must finally achieve the last and highest presuppositions, and then we can take them for themselves.
(Nelson [1904], p. 4f.)

Therefore, if we call the method [*Verfahren*] of a science *dogmatic* that starts from positing its principles, and the method of a science *critical* that examines even its principles, we can say that a critical method matters for philosophy, and that criticism in philosophy consists of the observance of the regressive method [*regressive Methode*].
(Nelson [1904], p. 7)

Nelson thus focuses on the role in philosophizing of the regressive method, which starts from ordinary experience and then achieves "the last and highest presuppositions" through the "analysis and abstraction" of particular given examples. He proceeds by comparing it with the progressive method, which starts from the first and highest principle and attempts to deduce lower principles from it. Nelson emphasizes the "actuality" of philosophical cognition to support Fries' philosophical method.

The mysticism of a Platonic way of apprehension on the one hand, and the evidence of sensible intuition on the other hand, must have given Aristotelians priority in science. However, in the perfect formation of theoretical natural science, radical self-observation must to some extent have led again to acknowledgment of the undeniable actuality of metaphysical presuppositions, and therefore renewed the question of the ground [*Grund*] of the possibilities of these presuppositions.
(Nelson [1904], p. 56f.)

As shown here, "the undeniable actuality of metaphysical presuppositions" should be acknowledged in "the perfect formation of theoretical natural science." In addition, Nelson focuses on the role of abstraction as a means to reveal philosophical cognition, and emphasizes the distinction between induction and abstraction from this perspective. Furthermore, he emphasizes the role of abstraction rather than induction in philosophy.[49]

Induction is not the way to necessary truths, but the way to the connection of necessary truths with incidents, because necessary truths construct the highest premises [*die höchsten Obersätze*] that are already *a priori* underlying [*zu Grunde liegen*] all induction by observations. The way to the necessary truths is rather *abstraction*.
(Nelson [1904], p. 7f.)

There are two different regressive methods; we must still distinguish the regressive method of *abstraction* from that of *induction*. Therefore, the analyzing method [*zergliedende Verfahren*] for the discovery of philosophical principles should be distinguished from all methods of verification – not only from the progressive way in mathematics, but also from the regressive one of induction.

(Nelson [1904], p. 9)

Thus, Nelson finds the crux of Fries' philosophy to be the discovery of philosophical cognition through abstraction and the establishment of metaphysics.

Fries, however, problematizes the justification (*Begründung*) of philosophical cognition discovered through abstraction. Nelson also focuses on the problem of justifying philosophical cognition.[50] He characterizes deduction in Fries' philosophy as only subjective justification:

However, how should we justify metaphysical principles? We cannot verify them, because in that case they would not be principles. On the other hand, they cannot be demonstrated, because in that case they would not be metaphysical. We call the way to justify them *deduction*. What then is the essence of deduction?

There is no other justification of a cognition than that through presentation [*Angabe*] of the immediate cognition from which the cognition is derived. The highest reasons [*Gründe*] consist of immediate cognition. However, all mediate cognition is cognition through concepts, i.e., judgments. Strictly speaking, we may require that not every cognition but only every judgment must have a reason [*Grund*], and all mediate [*mittelbar*] judgments are made in order to verify [*beweisen*]. All immediate judgments, however, are made either to deduce [*deduzieren*] or to demonstrate [*demonstrieren*]. This reason [*Grund*] can never be sought in relation to the object, but only in relation to the immediate cognition. What matters most is the distinction of the judgment's relationship with cognition from the cognition's relationship with the object.

(Nelson [1904], p. 22)

Nelson thus finds the means to justify metaphysical reasons in deduction. To illuminate the characteristics of deduction by emphasizing the similarity between deduction and demonstration, Nelson points out that all immediate judgments are made in order either "to deduce" (*deduzieren*) or "to demonstrate" (*demonstrieren*). He asserts that both demonstration and deduction lie in the "exhibition" of immediate cognition, and then thematizes the distinction between them.

Deduction coincides with demonstration insomuch as both methods serve the justification of basic judgments. Therefore, these operations consist of exhibiting [*Aufweisung*] immediate cognition, insomuch as they construct the grounds [*Grund*] of problematic judgment. However, judgments that are only deducible are not grounded in intuition like demonstrable judgments, i.e., we never become conscious of the immediate cognition that underlies the deducible [*deduzierbar*] judgments immediately, but only through the mediation of reflection, only through judgment. This condition constitutes the essential distinction between both ways, because while we can compare the intuition with the judgment immediately in the case of demonstration, we can make only a mediate comparison in that of deduction; the criterion for the validity of judgments is not immediately available as it is with demonstration, but rather it must be queried artificially and achieved in the first place.
(Nelson [1904], p. 22f.)

Here Nelson points out that the immediate cognition constructing metaphysical principles can be accomplished only through judgment and the mediation of reflection, in order to highlight the characteristics of deduction, which can be justified only through a mediate comparison; whereas in the case of demonstration we can immediately compare the intuition with the judgment. On the basis of this distinction between demonstration and deduction, Nelson emphasizes that deduction is characteristically related only to subjective justification,[51] in order to avoid "overestimating the demands on deduction":[52]

However, as the demonstrable truth is conspicuous rather than the deducible truth, because of its immediate evidence, we must remark that this priority is only restricted by the different relationship of both forms of cognition with consciousness, because in both cases the object cannot be referred to as a witness of truth. Therefore, so as not to overestimate the demands on deduction, the most important result of the inquiry is the indication that in demonstration we are concerned only with subjective justification and that, in spite of ordinary preoccupations, the certainty of the most evident truths can never be based on objective criteria like the truths of mathematical axioms.
(Nelson [1904], p. 23)

Nelson emphasizes the role of deduction as a justification of philosophical cognition, and reason (*Vernunft*) as a mental faculty that contains philosophical cognition as immediate cognition. He focuses on the concept of the self-confidence of reason (*das Selbstvertrauen der Vernunft*), and attempts to justify the role of psychology in his philosophy by emphasizing the necessity of reason as a mental faculty.

To comprehend this deduction, nothing is more important than its distinction from every art of verification. The critique of reason only inquires: Which immediate cognition does our reason [*Vernunft*] possess? Here, the self-confidence of reason, based on the truth [*Wahrheit*] of its immediate cognition, in general must be established as the highest premise of all deductions. Therefore, although the critique deduces metaphysical principles through a theory of reason [*Vernunft*] that can be gained through inner experience, i.e., only in the inductive way [*induktorisch*], the metaphysical principles are, according to its validity, based on neither experience nor induction, because they are not verified [*bewiesen*] by the theory of reason, but only exhibited [*aufgewiesen*] as such. Here, in answering the *quid juris* of these principles, the inference is not based on the underlying inductions of inner experience, but on the self-confidence of reason [*Selbstvertrauen der Vernunft*]. This self-confidence of reason is a general principle that turns psychological derivation by the theory of reason into critical deductions, i.e., that enables us to find guidance for the systematic justification of philosophy in the inner experience.

(Nelson [1904], p. 29)

Nelson focuses on the concept of the self-confidence of reason by emphasizing the problem of deduction as the justification of philosophical cognition. All developments in Nelson's philosophy are based on his reception of Fries', as discussed above, and this reception had a significant influence on the interpretation of Fries' philosophy by Nelson's contemporaries.[53] In fact, Wolfgang Röd claims that Nelson's argument about the justification of immediate cognition inspired Popper to develop his own philosophical standpoint by criticizing Fries' thought.[54]

3.2.3 The Neo-Friesian school's battle against Neo-Kantianism

This chapter explores the development of Leonard Nelson's thought and his critique of Neo-Kantian philosophers.

Neo-Kantian philosophers dominated the philosophical world in early–20th-century Germany. Some philosophical streams of thought, however, remained opposed to the Neo-Kantian movements, and there were philosophical debates between the two. One of the most outstanding groups was the Neo-Friesian school, which was established by Leonard Nelson early in the 20th century.

The chapter describes Nelson's critique of the Neo-Kantian philosophers in terms of the development of his philosophy. It first examines Nelson's attack, in his earliest papers, on Hermann Cohen's interpretation of Fries' philosophy. Second, this chapter examines Nelson's critique of Heinrich Rickert.[55]

3.2.3.1 Nelson's stance against Cohen's critique

As shown above, in his earliest papers Nelson began his reception of Fries' philosophy with a counter-critique of contemporary Neo-Hegelian and Neo-Kantian philosophers. Among them was Hermann Cohen, a Neo-Kantian philosopher of the so-called Marburg school. Nelson's criticism of Cohen in a paper of 1904 was so conspicuous and so drastic that Nelson failed to receive a doctoral degree as a result.[56]

Nelson's denunciation of Cohen was a response to Cohen's critique of Fries' thought as psychologism, which Cohen developed in his book *Kant's Theory of Experience*. In the second edition, in 1885, Cohen added a chapter titled "Fries' Anthropological Mistake." In that chapter, Cohen comments on Bona Meyer's philosophy, based on Fries,' and criticizes Fries for his psychological tendency in interpreting Kant.

> In this whole policy in which Bona Meyer vaporizes the meaning of the transcendental into the psychological, he follows Jacob Friedrich Fries. Meyer often acknowledges the "revision" of Kant that was made by Fries. Fries has complemented Kantian philosophy in an excellent way according to this side, i.e., in terms of the transcendental question. This side was conspicuous when compared to Herbart, who denies all the achievement [of Fries].
>
> (Cohen [1885], p. 296)

As this shows, Cohen criticized Fries' philosophy as an inaccurate transfiguration of Kant's transcendental philosophy into psychology, and called it an anthropological mistake, or psychologism. Cohen's critique of Fries' as a psychological interpretation of Kant was coincident with the appraisal of Fries made by Otto Liebmann, a proponent of Neo-Kantianism. Liebmann claimed that Fries regarded the Kantian critique as a psychological one, and he asserted that "it is the worst misunderstanding to regard it [Kantian critique] as a psychological one."[57] Liebmann concludes that Fries' philosophy was "no improvement on Kant's, but only a retrogression to Locke."

In addition, Cohen's critical interpretation of Fries was often related to the doctrines of the Friesian school's philosophers. The most striking of them was Ernst Friedrich Apelt, a proponent of the first Friesian school.

Cohen himself claimed that when he criticized Fries' interpretation of Kant's philosophy, "[w]e [Cohen] think of Jacob Friedrich Fries and his student Ernst Friedrich Apelt."[58]

Nelson's critique of the Neo-Kantian philosophers corresponds to the discussions noted here. According to Nelson, the gist of the Neo-Kantian philosophers' critique of Fries was that they identified it as a psychological interpretation of Kant:

> The Neo-Kantian school claims: "If the transcendental deduction might be characterized as an investigation belonging to psychology, the discipline of metaphysics in general would be dissolved into the discipline of psychology."[59]
>
> (Nelson [1904], p. 43)

Nelson, then, regards the Neo-Kantian reading of Fries as an interpretation according to which Fries characterizes transcendental deduction as an investigation belonging to psychology. From this viewpoint, Nelson begins his critique of the Neo-Kantian philosophers by claiming that they confuse apriority with apodicticity. He calls this confusion the Neo-Kantian philosophers' "preoccupation," and finds in it the cause of their underestimation of Fries' philosophy:

> Therefore, from this preoccupation [i.e., confusion between apriority and apodicticity], the great achievement of Fries' deductions appears [to Neo-Kantian philosophers] as a retrogression to *Locke's* empiricism. However, because this preoccupation leads to the consequence that the critique must be metaphysical, this preoccupation rather removes the basic thought of a critique of reason, and *eo ipso* the concept of criticism disappears and is immediately reduced to dogmatism.
> This very preoccupation makes it impossible for the Neo-Kantian school to go back to pure criticism.
>
> (Nelson [1904], p. 43)

Here Nelson finds the distinctive viewpoint of Fries' philosophy in the distinction between apriority and apodicticity, which, according to Nelson, Neo-Kantian philosophers overlook, causing them to fall into the very dogmatism which they attempt to avoid under the name of Kantian criticism. Nelson then moves to "focus on Cohen's attack against the 'anthropological mistake' [...] of the supporter of the psychological critique [i.e., Fries]."[60]

To respond to Cohen's critique of Fries, Nelson develops a series of arguments. One of the most striking of those was a debate regarding the concept of transcendental apperception. According to Nelson, Cohen says of Fries that "this apprehension of transcendental apperception itself shows its insufficiency, because Fries needs a formal apperception for its complement."[61] Nelson points out that Cohen's interpretation is inappropriate because Cohen overlooks the difference between Kant's and Fries' understanding of this word:

> However, in addition, the claim is totally false that Fries has introduced formal apperception as a complement of transcendental apperception, because in the case of Fries formal apperception means nothing but what Kant vaguely calls the unity of transcendental apperception (J.F. Fries. *Neue Kritik der Vernunft.* § 93).
>
> (Nelson [1904], p. 82)

Nelson also responds to Cohen's critique of Apelt's philosophy. As shown above, Cohen attacked Apelt's interpretation of Fries' philosophy, and the conflict between the Neo-Kantians and the Neo-Friesians was oriented toward the first Friesian school's philosophy. Nelson also attempts to defend Apelt:

> Following the accomplishment of this execution [i.e., Cohen's misinterpretation of Fries' philosophy], unlucky Apelt was bound to the procrustean bed of Cohen's logic of interpretation. "Apelt makes this transcendental and formal apperception the speculative basic form of all metaphysical cognition." Where had Apelt offended such a fool? Otherwise, I cannot account for the conceptual distortion that Cohen inflicted on Apelt, because this distortion is absolutely nonsense for everyone who clearly knows to any extent what *Apelt* understands under the words "transcendental apperception," "formal apperception" and "speculative basic form."
>
> (Nelson [1904], p. 84)

Nelson here reduces Cohen's critique of Apelt to a misreading. As shown above, the development of Nelson's thought began with a defense of Fries' philosophy and the assertion that it was not psychologism. In this sense, Nelson's critique of Cohen's philosophy was accomplished through his interpretation of Fries' philosophy.

3.2.3.2 *Nelson's critique of Rickert's views*

3.2.3.2.1 EMPHASIS ON THE IMPOSSIBILITY OF THE THEORY OF COGNITION

In 1908's *On the So-called Problem of Cognition*, Nelson began to state his own perspective in comparison to the contemporary debate, under the name of the "theory of cognition" (*Erkenntnistheorie*). In this book, Nelson gives the gist of his argument a new formulation. He calls it "the impossibility of the theory of cognition." The title of the first chapter is "General Proof of the Impossibility of the Theory of Cognition."[62] In that chapter, Nelson declares the book's theme:

> The *theory of cognition* is – according to common use of this word – the science that takes as its task the investigation of the objective validity of cognition in general. To posit this task presupposes that the objective validity of cognition is doubtful, i.e., that the existence of objective validity creates a problem. Now, I claim that a scientific resolution of this problem is *impossible*.
>
> (Nelson [1908], p. 32)

In the book Nelson thematizes his conception of the "theory of cognition," which signifies "the science that makes the investigation of the objective validity of cognition in general as its task." He attempts to explain his own standpoint, using the term "theory of cognition" as a key phrase to signify a target of his critiques, and he formulates this standpoint by criticizing contemporary philosophical trends.

> The contradiction [of the biological form of the theory of cognition] illuminated above is not particular to the biological form of the theory of cognition. Rather, because of this contradiction every attempt must fail that aims to solve [the problem of] cognition's independence and particular form of *objectivity* and to reduce them to another matter.
>
> (Nelson [1908], p. 80)

3.2.3.2.2 CRITIQUE OF RICKERT'S STANDPOINT

Unlike Nelson's earliest papers, where his target was Cohen's interpretation of Fries' philosophy, in his 1908 book Nelson rarely refers to Cohen's argument. Instead, among his contemporaries, Nelson aims his critiques at Rickert, Lipps, and Natorp's Neo-Kantian movement, as well as Husserl's phenomenology. In Nelson's central argument regarding the impossibility of the theory of cognition, the target lies in Nelson's critique of Rickert's argument.

Rickert attempts to defend the justification of the objectivity (*Begründung der Objektivität*) of our cognition.[63] By criticizing that position, Nelson attempts to justify his rejection of the theory of cognition, and to restrict the validity of cognition to the subjective. Referring to the second edition of Rickert's *Object of Cognition* (*Der Gegenstand der Erkenntnis*) in 1904,

The Friesian and Neo-Friesian schools 81

Nelson targets Rickert's conception of the justification of our cognition's objectivity and the concept of a transcendent "ought" (*transzendentes Sollen*),[64] which Rickert thinks are grounds to justify the objectivity of our cognition. Nelson claims that "Rickert's 'ought' [*Sollen*] is in fact a requirement whose concept is required by nobody,"[65] and therefore this concept does not make sense.

Nelson also examines Rickert's concept of the will, and claims that Rickert confused the subjective nature of our mental faculty with logical necessity without being aware of it. Consequently, according to Nelson, Rickert himself falls into the psychologism that he himself criticizes.

> Therefore, the criterion of Rickert's theory of cognition should be found in the impossibility of contradiction; i.e., surely in logical necessity, therefore in what should first be justified through this theory. Therefore, according to Rickert, "psychologism" necessarily leads to a cycle. If so, Rickert's "psychologism" itself does so before all others, because Rickert's theory of cognition *is* psychologism, if we have a right to call "psychologism" the confusion of the real grounds for forming a judgment with the logical grounds of its truth.
> (Nelson [1908], S. 143)

In addition, Nelson claims that Rickert disguises the psychological phenomenon of our mental activity as logical necessity because Rickert overlooked the precise distinction between them.

> Without the psychological observation of judgment's dependence on the will, Rickert could never have come to introduce the will into his theory of cognition, although he surely must have denied the psychological nature of this observation afterwards in order to avoid the appearance of psychologism. In addition, the proposition of judgment's dependence on the will, which is in itself correct, cannot thoroughly be based on the criterion Rickert claims, that "contradiction lies in its denial." The denial of this proposition can be made without any contradiction; the proposition can never be based on so-called logical necessity, but absolutely on psychological observation. However, what psychological observation here means is not a dependence of *cognition in general* on the will, but only such a dependence of cognition through *judgment*; so for this reason the proposition of the will as the "ultimate foundation of cognition" is false.[66]
> (Nelson [1908], p. 143)

As already mentioned, Nelson's earliest paper already claimed that Fries "was never a psychologist, but rather he fought against the psychologism of his contemporaries most drastically, and investigated the true salvation for philosophy's progression [*Fortbildung*] in freeing it from psychologism."[67] As an example of Fries' fight against psychologism, Nelson refers to Fries' critique of Reinhold and Fichte (and Schelling in his earliest period). Fries criticizes them by pointing out that they adopt a progressive, or synthetic, method that starts from a first principle. He claims that Reinhold and Fichte regard the products of self-observation of inner experiences as a metaphysical first principle and, therefore, confuse merely psychological cognition with such a metaphysical first principle. According to Nelson, Fries' critique of the German idealists shows his attempt to avoid confusion between psychological and philosophical cognition,[68] and to distinguish them from each other.

In this sense, Nelson finds in his attack against Rickert a repetition of the battle between Fries and the German idealism of Reinhold and Fichte. Considering the historical background in which the Neo-Kantian philosophical movement arose from the Neo-Hegelian movement as a final stage of German idealism, and considering too that the thoughts of the Baden school's philosophers like Rickert and Windelband are often characterized as Neo-Fichteanism,[69] it might be accurate of Nelson to say that he criticized Rickert's standpoint as one representative of the Neo-Kantian philosophical movement, while he also focused on Fichte's philosophy and exhaustively criticized it in the same book in 1908.

3.2.3.3 Conclusion

This section has addressed Nelson's critique of Neo-Kantian philosophers, especially Hermann Cohen and Heinrich Rickert. It first examined Nelson's attack in his earliest papers on Hermann Cohen's interpretation of Fries. Second, the section focused on Nelson's schematization of the impossibility of the theory of cognition in 1908, and on Nelson's critique of Heinrich Rickert's key conception of the theory of cognition in defense of his own views.

As shown above, the debate between Nelson, as a philosopher of the Neo-Friesian school, and philosophers of the Neo-Kantian school contains diverse aspects corresponding to the development of Nelson's own philosophy. Nelson's attacks against Neo-Kantian philosophers reflect the milieu of 20th-century philosophers.

3.2.4 The Neo-Friesian school and the analytic tradition

This chapter attempts to reevaluate the historical significance of Nelson's thought and the Neo-Friesian school's activity, in order to bridge the

The Friesian and Neo-Friesian schools 83

historical gap between the Post-Kantian tradition in the 19th century and that of analytic philosophy in the 20th century.

As already seen, the Neo-Friesian school was a philosophical movement founded by Nelson in the early 20th century in Göttingen. In 1904, Nelson began his philosophical activity by defending Fries' thought from attacks by Hegelians, such as Fischer, and by reevaluating Fries' philosophy. In this sense, the Neo-Friesian school arose as an alternative to Hegelianism, and Nelson's defense of Fries' philosophy illuminated hidden philosophical options outside the Hegelian tradition in Post-Kantian thought.

The circle of the Neo-Friesian school in Göttingen expanded to include some significant mathematicians and logicians known as logical empiricists, such as Kurt Grelling. Nelson's philosophy and the activity of the Neo-Friesian school bear not only a historical relationship with early contributors to the analytic philosophy movement, but also philosophical affinities with the characteristics of the analytic tradition.

In light of these congruities, this chapter examines Nelson's philosophy and its milieu in consideration of the history of 19th- and early–20th-century philosophy. It explores the similarity of Nelson's philosophy to the tradition of analytic philosophy, as well as the historical relationship between them, and attempts to respond to a negative interpretation in previous research by focusing on Nelson's conception of the Socratic method.

3.2.4.1 Historical relationship to analytic philosophy

As the previous chapter showed, the entire conception of Nelson's philosophy is based on the reception of Fries' philosophy in Nelson's earliest period. In consequence, Nelson's central conception of philosophy gained a character easily distinguished from the contemporary movement of Neo-Kantian philosophy. Recent studies have focused on the relationship of Nelson's philosophy to the early traditions of analytic philosophy.[70] The following section examines the characteristics of Nelson's philosophical standpoint that display similarities to analytic philosophy.

The first similarity to the analytic tradition in Nelson's thought can be found in his philosophical method. As shown above, Nelson claims, following Fries' views, that we humans adopt philosophical principles in all our judgments and opinions without being conscious of them. From this viewpoint, Nelson identifies the task of philosophy with the analysis and abstraction of our daily judgments and opinions.[71] He finds the method of philosophy in the regressive method, which is also called the analytic method. As already seen, Nelson's analytic method was based on the reception of Fries' philosophy as a form of resistance to the Hegelian movement. This confrontation with Hegelianism gave rise to Nelson's essential philosophic position and his identification of the method of philosophy with the analytic method, as the way to accomplish analysis of our daily judgments and opinions. This in turn laid a foundation for the methodological standpoint of the tradition of analytic philosophy. This should be distinguished from the philosophical scheme of Neo-Kantianism and phenomenology as a prominent mode of thought in the early 20th century.

The second similarity is found in Nelson's critique of foundationalism regarding philosophical cognition. He criticizes the view that requires ultimate justification of cognition, labeling it a theory of cognition. Nelson emphasizes the impossibility of finding an ultimate justification of our philosophical cognition in an objective way, and the necessity of abandoning such an attempt. He claims that the ultimate justification of our philosophical cognition can be accomplished only in a subjective way, insomuch as it can be justified through deduction, i.e., by the exhibition of its coincidence with immediate cognition in reason. Nelson calls his own claim the impossibility of the theory of cognition, and exaggerates his position by criticizing contemporary philosophical movements such as Neo-Kantianism. He claims that Neo-Kantianism, like Rickert's philosophy, is under the illusion that all philosophical cognition should be objectively justified. He posits his own theory, based on his reception of Fries' philosophy, against the contemporary Neo-Kantian movement.

Nelson's thought had a significant influence on the formation of the stream of thought constituting analytic philosophy and philosophy of science. First, his idea of the impossibility of a theory of cognition is known for its influence on Popper's philosophy. It is well known that Popper examined Fries' philosophical views precisely in his manuscript,[72] and then in his main work formulated the problem of justification into Fries' Trilemma.[73] According to Milkov, Popper knew Nelson's philosophy through Julius Kraft, who wrote his doctoral dissertation under Nelson.[74] Citing Popper's autobiography, Milkov explains that Kraft and Nelson had endless face-to-face discussions from 1924 to 1926,[75] and that about half of these were about Kant's so-called transcendental deduction, his solution to the antinomies, and Nelson's ideas about the impossibility of a theory of knowledge.[76]

Furthermore, at the beginning of the 20th century philosophers known as logical empiricists, such as Kurt Grelling, also belonged to the Neo-Friesian school, and influenced contemporary trends in logic. In this sense, Nelson's philosophy provides the missing link between Hegelian thought in the 19th century and the analytic tradition of the 20th century.

3.2.4.2 *The object of philosophy according to Nelson: Linguistic analysis as a method of philosophizing*

As described above, Nelson's philosophy developed out of a perspective distinct from contemporary movements like Neo-Kantianism and the early phenomenology of the period. This characteristic of his philosophy reveals an affinity with the analytic tradition, both in key methodological concepts like the analytic method and in the historical background relating to the activity of the Neo-Friesian school.

However, analytic philosophy's similarities to Nelson's thought have often been questioned. For example, Glock focuses on the linguistic turn as a characteristic of the analytic tradition, and remarks on the interesting parallelism[77] between the concept of Socratic dialogue in Nelson's philosophy and the analytic tradition's, or specifically Wittgenstein's, philosophical standpoint. Glock mentions, though, that Nelson made no linguistic turn comparable to Wittgenstein's *Tractatus* or the Vienna Circle because Nelson's general methodological interest in philosophy in language is limited to propaedeutic warnings, and Nelson seems not to regard these warnings as especially revolutionary.[78]

Glock's interpretation of Nelson's philosophy, however, underestimates the role of Socratic dialogue and the Socratic method in it. In other words, Glock overlooks the fact that the Socratic method is a philosophical method that Nelson formalized to identify the object of philosophy with our use of language.

It is remarkable that Fries himself had already identified the object of philosophy with our use of language, insomuch as he identified the object of philosophizing with the mental act of "having opinions" (*Beurteilung*). Fries' philosophical method is oriented through this identification of the object of philosophy with "having opinions." Conversely, in Nelson's reception of Fries' philosophy, Nelson seems to overlook the importance of "opinions" for Fries' position. Nelson did, however, attempt to formulate another position supporting Fries' point with the concept of an opinion; Nelson focuses on the role of dialogue as a way to reveal the general presuppositions of our opinions, which seem *prima facie* various and plural.

Fries himself had already used the term "consensus-building" (*Verständigung*)[79] to characterize his philosophical method: The discovery and clarification of the philosophical cognitions that construct the general presuppositions of our daily opinions. He, however, did not make the concept of consensus building a central motive of his philosophy. Nelson attempts to emphasize the role of dialogue as a method of philosophizing, insomuch as what can at first be given to philosophy in a comprehensible way is language (*Sprache*) as a signifier of concepts through words;[80] he names his philosophical method the Socratic method. The following section examines the role of the Socratic method in Nelson's philosophy.

3.2.4.3 The Socratic method as a means of linguistic analysis

3.2.4.3.1 OUTLINE OF THE SOCRATIC METHOD

As already seen, Nelson's reception of Fries' philosophy focuses on abstraction as a means to reveal philosophical cognition, and on the self-confidence of reason as a justification of philosophical cognition.

After his earliest works, Nelson began to attempt to combine his philosophical thoughts with the idea of the Socratic method.[81] He tried to strengthen his philosophical position by aligning it with Socrates' name, and investigated a way to discover metaphysical principles through the so-called Socratic method. Nelson regards this combination as his own achievement, claiming that Fries did not and could not find the Socratic method in the method of Socrates himself,[82] and that Fries ignored the Socratic method.

Previous studies considered Nelson's Socratic method only in the context of ethics, and Nelson himself often examines the Socratic method by focusing on ethical contexts:

> Induction is the method of the natural scientist [*Naturforscher*]. However, it is known that *Socrates* did not share the effort of natural scientists in his period, and it is also known that by his method he did not aim to expand knowledge, but rather aimed to bring [*erheben*] knowledge that we already possess into the clarity of consciousness. In his work he started from opinions [*Beurteilung*] about a concrete case to bring the obscure and underlying general presuppositions into consciousness by proving the grounds [*Gründe*] of these opinions.
>
> (Nelson [1915], p. 29)[83]

As shown above, Nelson finds in Socrates' practice the way of philosophizing that Nelson learned from Fries' standpoint: "To bring [*erheben*] knowledge that we already possess into the clarity of the consciousness." On the contrary, the observation that "Socrates did not share the effort of natural scientists" might result in an ordinary understanding that regards the Socratic method as one only valid in the context of ethics and that distinguishes it from other scientific activities.

Nelson, however, also suggests that the Socratic method is valid in the discovery of the metaphysical principles that are presupposed in the *natural sciences*, by indicating the continuity between metaphysical and ethical principles:

It is astonishing how this simple methodological thought is misunderstood even now. For example, it is claimed that it is only Socrates' practical interest in the ethical awakening of his neighbors that is expressed in relation to the issues of daily life. No, it is not. Even if Socrates were a natural philosopher rather than a moralist [*Ethiker*], he would have accomplished his speculation in the same way.

(Nelson [1915], p. 24)

Therefore, it becomes necessary to address why Nelson focuses on ethical issues in the context of the Socratic method. The following section argues that he does so only to emphasize the distinction between induction and abstraction, and that he regards the discovery of scientific principles and ethical ones as interwoven.

3.2.4.3.2 THE DISTINCTION BETWEEN INDUCTION AND ABSTRACTION

Nelson's goal in focusing on the context of ethics is to distinguish between induction and abstraction. He claims that it is Aristotle who confused the two.

Aristotle – and historians of philosophy following him – praise *Socrates* by claiming that he was the discoverer of induction. Therefore, in Aristotelian Logic, the regressive inference from the particular to the general [*vom Besonderen auf das Allgemeine*] is, under the name of induction, opposed to the progressive inference from the general to the particular [...]. Indeed, the famous "Socratic method" is a regression from the particular to the general. However, it is not induction. Its transition from the particular to the general is not performed through inference, but through analysis [*Zergliederung*].

(Nelson [1915], p. 28)

This method [abstraction] was already found by Socrates and Plato. However, Aristotle confused the Socratic method of abstraction with induction under the name of ἐπαγωγή. This misunderstanding remained in the history of philosophy until Kant.

(Nelson [1904], p. 10)

As shown, Nelson attempts to ascribe the method of abstraction to Socrates, by claiming that Aristotle, being engaged in the field of natural science, confused abstraction with induction (cf. Nelson [1915], p. 29). Nelson focuses here on the context of ethics only because ethics is the field of inquiry in which abstraction can be most distinctly differentiated from induction.

Furthermore, Nelson identifies the way to discover ethical principles with the means of discovering metaphysical ones, indicating the methods' congruity.

> For example, to find the principles of calculation, we must use abstraction. Everyone makes use of these principles in concrete cases. However, to become conscious of these principles in their general form requires the analysis [*Zergliederung*] of a certain operation of calculation. When we have to add a series of numbers, we summate it again in a reversed way in order to prove the result. If we seek what justifies this proving operation, we find it in the presupposition that the amount of the sum is independent of the series of its terms. This proposition is a principle of arithmetic, but not a theorem. It cannot be verified, but only exhibited [*aufweisen*] as such. [...] It is the same also in ethics. When we doubt whether we hurt another person by a certain mode of behavior, we think, put ourselves in the place of another person, and ask whether we might feel pain from such a behavior in that place. If we investigate under which presupposition we are behaving, we find it in the proposition that the ethical value of a behavior is independent of the exchanging of the persons who are interacting with each other. This proposition here is not verified, but only exhibited as a presupposition of another proposition. Furthermore, a single example is sufficient for this exhibition.
>
> (Nelson [1915], p. 30)

Through this emphasis on the context of ethics, Nelson attempts to claim that it was abstraction that Socrates really investigated, while Aristotle confused abstraction with induction. In this sense, Nelson does not attempt to restrict the validity of the Socratic method to the context of ethics, but rather ensures its validity in both metaphysical and ethical contexts by ascribing the method of abstraction to the Socratic method. Therefore, the discovery of ethical principles through the Socratic method operates in parallel with that of metaphysical ones.

3.2.4.4 Conclusion

This chapter has examined the similarity of Nelson's philosophical standpoint to the tradition of analytic philosophy in relation to his conception of the Socratic method. It explored both this similarity and the historical relationship between Nelson's philosophy and the analytic tradition, and attempted to respond to Glock's negative interpretation by focusing on Nelson's conception of the Socratic method.

The Friesian and Neo-Friesian schools 89

As shown above, Nelson's philosophy plays the role of a bridge between the traditions of analytic philosophy and Post-Kantian continental philosophy through the similarity of its methodological viewpoint to the analytic tradition's. In this sense, Nelson's philosophy provides a missing link between continental thought in 19th-century Germany and the analytic tradition in the 20th century.

Notes

1 Cf. Herrmann [2000], p. 20.
2 Kay Hermann points out that various natural scientists – such as Oskar Schlömilch, C. Grapengießer, Matthias Jacob Schleiden, Ernst Sigismund Mirbt, and Eduard Oscar Schmidt – belonged to the Friesian school (Hermann [2000], p. 206).
3 Apelt [1847], p. 3.
4 Ibid., p. 4f.
5 Ibid., p. 6.
6 Apelt [1857], p. VII.
7 Cf. Apelt [1854], p. V; Herrmann [2000], p. 207.
8 This information is based on the *Internet Encyclopedia of Philosophy*, "Rudolf Hermann Lotze (1817–1881)" (9 November 2018).
9 Cf. Eggeling [1875]; Zeltner [1953].
10 Cf. Herrmann [2000], p. 207.
11 NKV, I, p. 320ff.; NaKV, I, p. 381ff. Because of this description, many researchers have understood that Fries adopts induction as a central method of philosophizing.
12 This distinction by Fries is also explained by Leonard Nelson (cf. Nelson [1904], pp. 3–14).
13 NKV, I, p. 326; NaKV, I, p. 389.
14 SM, p. 185.
15 This claim is repeated in Fries' *System of Logic*: "Speculation is concerned with the exhibition of the general rules [*Allgemeine Regeln*]. Although we are not conscious of these rules, we presuppose them as truths in our [...] philosophical opinions [*Beurteilung*]. Conversely, [...] induction leads to a regressive verification to general laws by ordering phenomena under prescriptive maxims" (SL, p. 562).
16 Bonnet [2013] offers an explanation of Fries and Apelt's distinction between induction and speculation (Bonnet [2013], p. 110ff.).
17 Cf. Apelt [1854], p. 71f.
18 Ibid., p. 56f.
19 Ibid., p. 65.
20 Ibid., p. 69.
21 Popper [1935], p. 61.
22 Bonnet [2013] examines Popper's reaction to Fries' philosophy in *The Two Fundamental Problems of the Theory of Knowledge*, but does not focus on Popper's reference to Apelt's discussion. Cf. Bonnet [2013], p. 267.
23 Apelt [1857], p. VIII.
24 Ibid.
25 Ibid., p. 21.

26 Ibid., p. VII.
27 Apelt [1857], p. 535.
28 Apelt [1857], pp. VII, 534; Röd [1996], p. 191.
29 Röd [1996], p. 191.
30 Apelt [1857], p. 509.
31 Apelt connects this concept of "re-consciousness" with Plato's conception of "recollection" (ἀνάμνησις) to authorize his standpoint within the history of philosophy (Apelt [1857], p. 209). Röd comments as follows: "Although Apelt regarded [Plato's] expression of 'recollection' as a metaphor [...], he also thought the core of the theory of recollection to be legitimate" (Röd [1996], p. 191). Roberto [2007], in accordance with Cassirer's reference to Fries' philosophy, illuminates this aspect as a characteristic of Fries' own views. Cf. Roberto [2007], p. 111f.
32 Cassirer [1920], p. 475.
33 Cassirer [1920], p. 482.
34 Hermut Pulte summarizes critiques of Fries after Apelt's death as follows:
    While Fries' efforts to reconcile philosophy, mathematics and the sciences received positive feedback with his contemporaries, the later reception of his work was less favourable. First of all, mainly because of a politically motivated interdiction to teach, Fries himself failed to set up a philosophical school. What is more, his most eminent disciple, E.F. Apelt (1812–1859), suffered an untimely death. Therefore the (first) "Friesian school," spearheaded by that latter scholar, was a philosophical flash in the pan. In addition, the reception of Fries' work within academic philosophy suffered from the dominance of German Idealism (especially Hegel and his adherents), to which his philosophy was opposed. Later, Neo-Kantianism and its imperative of going straight "Back to Kant" led to a disregard of post-Kantian developments, even if they stood in close relation to his work. For these reasons and others, mainly rooted in the problematic German historiography of philosophy and the sciences [...], Fries' attempt to bring philosophy and science together was poorly received in the later nineteenth and early twentieth century, outside of the New Friesian School. (Pulte [2013], p. 48)
35 For example, Jahn [1991] examines the relationship between Fries and Schleiden by focusing on Schleiden's lecture and its relation to Fries' *Handbuch der psychischen Anthropologie*.
36 Cassirer [1950], p. 157.
37 Cf. Herrmann [2000], p. 21.
38 Gerhard Hessenberg and Karl Kaiser participated in this meeting (Herrmann [2000], p. 21).
39 Kay Hermann points out that various natural scientists – such as Otto Apelt, Otto Berg, Paul Bernays, Ernst Fraenkel, Kurt Grelling, Gerhard Hessenberg, Arthur Kronfeld, Otto Meyerhof, and Rudolf Otto – belonged to the Friesian school (ibid.).
40 Cf. Blencke [1978], p. 205.
41 Kay Herrmann mentions Alexander Rüstow, Karl Brinkmann, and Heinrich Goesch. In addition, David Hilbert became an honorary member of this association in 1913 (Blencke [1978], p. 206).
42 Cf. Herrmann [2011], p. 2ff.
43 Nelson's attitude toward Apelt was so ambiguous that Nelson's interpretation of Fries' philosophy includes significant differences from Apelt's (cf. Pulte [2013],

The Friesian and Neo-Friesian schools 91

p. 47), while Nelson showed considerable respect to Apelt as a proponent of the Friesian school (Nelson [1904], p. 71f).
44 Nelson [1905], p. 257.
45 Ibid., p. 254.
46 Ibid., p. 293.
47 Ibid., p. 296.
48 Cf. Nelson [1904], p. 24.
49 Cf. Nelson [1905], p. 272.
50 This problem is especially central in Nelson [1908]; Nelson [1912]. Wolfgang Röd also finds the distinctive points of Nelson's interpretation of Fries' philosophy in his emphasis on the problem of justification (cf. Röd [1996], p. 193).
51 The nature of deduction as subjective justification can be found already in Fries' own views. Beiser emphasizes this aspect of Fries' deduction. Cf. Beiser [2014], p. 75.
52 Nelson [1904], p. 23.
53 Cf. Nelson [1908], p. 31ff.
54 Cf. Röd [1996], p. 193.
55 The Neo-Friesian school is often regarded as a component of the Neo-Kantian movements. From this perspective, the battle between the Neo-Friesian school and the Neo-Kantian schools is also often regarded as an internal conflict between Neo-Kantian schools. However, the Neo-Friesian school should be regarded as a movement independent from the Neo-Kantian schools for the following reasons: First, the activity of the Neo-Friesian school was not based on the immediate reception and interpretation of Kant's philosophy, but rather on the immediate reception of Fries' philosophy. Second, the development of Nelson's thought did not arise from any Neo-Kantian school's activities, but rather began with antagonism against the contemporaneous dominance of the Neo-Kantian schools. Third, in contrast to the Neo-Kantian schools, many natural scientists like biologists, and mathematicians and logicians as well, were involved in the activity of the Neo-Friesian school. In this sense, the Neo-Friesian school is not a branch of the Neo-Kantian movement but rather an independent movement of the same period.
56 Francke [1991], p. 74.
57 Liebmann [1865], p. 151.
58 Cohen [1885], p. 373.
59 These sentences appear in Cohen [1885], p. 294.
60 Nelson [1904], p. 43.
61 Ibid., p. 82.
62 Nelson [1908], p. 32.
63 Rickert [1904], p. 125.
64 Ibid.
65 Nelson [1908], p. 83.
66 From this perspective, Nelson summarizes Rickert's failure as follows:
    Therefore, Rickert's justification of this proposition includes a triple confusion: 1) He commits a psychological confusion of judgment's dependence on the will with the so-called dependence of all *cognition* on the will; 2) he confuses the factual-psychological nature of the proposition of judgment's dependence on the will with a logical necessity; and 3) he confuses the cause of the judgment's formation with the ground of its validity (Nelson [1908], p. 143).
67 Nelson [1905], p. 257.

92 The Friesian and Neo-Friesian schools

68 Ibid., p. 254.
69 Heidegger [1987], p. 142; Redaelli [2016], p. 3.
70 Berger [2011], p. 22.
71 Nelson [1904], p. 4.
72 Popper [1979], p. 113ff.
73 Popper [1935], p. 61.
74 Milkov [2012], p. 146.
75 Ibid., p. 146.
76 Ibid.
77 Glock [2011], p. 56
78 Ibid.
79 SM, p. 89.
80 Nelson [1915], p. 48.
81 Nelson already claims in his earliest work that "criticism has its origin only through Socrates and Kant" (Nelson [1904], p. 66).
82 Nelson [1931], p. 51.
83 Nelson emphasizes the difference between natural science and ethics by focusing on the distinction between being (*Sein*) and "ought" (*Sollen*) (cf. Nelson [1915], p. 31).

4 Conclusion

This book has examined Jakob Friedrich Fries', the Friesian school's and the Neo-Friesian school's philosophy from a methodological viewpoint, in order to illuminate this forgotten stream of thought in the reception and further development of Immanuel Kant's philosophy.

The schematization of 19th-century German philosophy has hitherto been under the influence of Hegelianism and Neo-Kantianism, such that any philosophical stream of thought other than so-called German idealism had no place in the orthodox history of philosophy. In response, this book has attempted to illuminate the thought of Fries and the Friesian and Neo-Friesian schools, which constituted a particular philosophical movement in the 19th and early 20th centuries.

The first chapter gave an overview of the historical background of Fries' philosophy and how his thought has been appraised. His standpoint has been regarded as psychologism. This estimation of Fries' philosophy originated with Herbart's description of it, following which Fischer and Erdmann, significant Hegelian philosophers, characterized Fries' standpoint with respect to psychology and anthropology, exaggerated his distance from Kant and German idealism, and presented Fries' views as a marginal trend. Liebmann and Windelband, significant Neo-Kantian philosophers, followed Fischer's estimation, characterized Fries' thought as psychologism, and purged him from the legitimate history of philosophy. However, it is a distortion to regard Fries' standpoint as psychologism. Fries' philosophy was not regarded as psychologism before his death, and an accurate comprehension of it appears in Schopenhauer and Hegel's interpretations.

In the second chapter, this book examined Fries' philosophy from this viewpoint. It first offered an overview of Fries' project of a critique of reason, i.e., the problem of the method of philosophy. Fries finds Kant's achievement in the thematization of philosophy, and Kant's problem in a defect in Kant's philosophical method. Accordingly, Fries based his standpoint on a correction of the method of philosophy following the influence of

94 Conclusion

Kant. Fries locates the way to philosophize in the discovery of philosophical cognition as the presuppositions of our ordinary opinions in daily life through analysis of those opinions, naming this the regressive method or the analytic method. Furthermore, he identifies the mental faculty that contains philosophical cognition with reason, and finds justification of philosophical cognition in the exhibition of the coincidence of those philosophical cognitions with the immediate cognition of reason, which Fries names deduction. He calls his whole project the critique of reason.

However, Fries' insight that *a priori* philosophical principles can be acquired through empirical cognition, and that transcendental cognition itself is empirical, was criticized by Hegelian and Neo-Kantian philosophers. Fischer, for example, objected to Fries by claiming in his 1862 lecture that what is *a priori* can never be cognized *a posteriori*. Nelson, a Neo-Friesian philosopher, attempted to answer Fischer's critique by drawing a distinction between the object of critique and the content of critique. However, because Fischer's critique questions the validity of this distinction itself, Nelson's argument is not a plausible response. This book therefore sought to answer this critique by noting the development of Fries' method of philosophy. The significant difference between Fries' earliest and later periods is found in the fact that, while in Fries' earliest paper he finds the object of philosophizing merely in ordinary experience, in the *New Critique of Reason* he identifies the object of philosophizing with "ordinary opinions [*gemeine Beurteilung*] in daily life." This led Fries to distinguish two mental faculties: Reason and understanding. In this sense, Fries had already attempted to answer the point of Fischer's critique in a different way from Nelson's response. In addition, Fries attempted to avoid psychologism by restricting the role of psychology.

The development of Fries' philosophy shown above was linked to his object of critique. In his earliest period, he found his standpoint in the regressive method and identified his object of critique with Fichte's conception of intellectual intuition, which led to the progressive or synthetic method. In his *New Critique of Reason*, in contrast, Fries found the object of philosophizing in ordinary opinions in daily life instead of in ordinary experience, and this led Fries to introduce a precise distinction between forms of abstraction: Quantitative abstraction and qualitative abstraction. He now found his object of critique in Schelling rather than Fichte, and criticized Schelling by examining his method of abstraction.

This book next addressed the development of key concepts in Fries' philosophy and the formation of his metaphysics. Among these concepts was that of the feeling of truth. While he finds the way to justify philosophical cognition in deduction, Fries introduces the concept of the feeling of truth as another criterion for the justification of philosophical cognition. This book investigated the role of this concept in accordance with its development, and illustrated Fries' intention of expanding the object of philosophy. In the *New Critique of Reason*, Fries finds the object of philosophy in the metaphysical principles of natural science, such as substance or causality, and also attempts to approach ethical principles by analogy with metaphysical ones.

In this period, Fries did not focus on the role of the feeling of truth. However, after the *New Critique of Reason*, he attempted to expand the object of philosophy. In his *Knowledge, Belief, and Aesthetic Sense*, Fries divides our cognition into *knowledge*, concerned with the metaphysical principles presupposed by our perceptual cognition; *belief*, concerned with the ethical principles presupposed by our moral judgment; and *aesthetic sense*, concerned with beauty and sublimity. As his conception of this division developed, Fries attempted to thematize ethical issues as ones independent from metaphysics, and to distinguish the methodology of the former from that of the latter; with this came a change in the role of the feeling of truth.

In addition to the feeling of truth, this book examined the role of the thing in itself in Fries' philosophy. While he seemed to concede the existence of the thing in itself on the one hand – which showed the distance of Fries' philosophy from German idealism and was therefore exaggerated by many researchers – on the other hand Fries denied the possibility of the thing in itself with respect to the concept of truth. This book examined this ambiguity in Fries' statements regarding the concept of the thing in itself in order to shed light on his aim to exaggerate his own standpoint. When Fries denies the possibility of the thing in itself, by this concept he symbolizes the standpoint that confuses things in themselves with appearances. Fries associated this standpoint with the German idealists who acknowledge the faculty of intellectual intuition, and he aimed to criticize them by denying the possibility of the thing in itself. To the contrary, when he conceded the existence of the thing in itself, he renamed it the "essence of things" or the "being of things in themselves." He regarded the relation between the appearance and the thing in itself as the relation between the apparent way of things and the essence of things, and reconceptualized them as two aspects of the same thing. As shown above, Fries reconstructed the concept of the thing in itself in order to introduce his own system, and distinguished his own standpoint from German idealism.

The third chapter addressed the activity of the Friesian and Neo-Friesian schools. It first examined the Friesian school established by Apelt, a student of Fries. Apelt attempted to bridge the gap between philosophy and contemporaneous natural science. He focused on the role of induction in his *Theory of Induction*, while he also emphasized the continuity between philosophy and mathematics regarding the justification of cognition by focusing on the nature of the immediate cognition of reason in his *Metaphysics*. These characteristics of Apelt's philosophy also influenced contemporaneous natural scientists such as Schleiden, a member of the Friesian school who emphasized the significance of Fries' philosophy in botany and examined the role of abstraction in botanical investigation.

Next, this book examined the activity of the Neo-Friesian school established by Nelson. Nelson's circle included mathematicians and logicians such as David Hilbert, Paul Bernays, and Kurt Grelling. Nelson's reception of Fries' philosophy is based on the philosophical method developed in Fries' earlier period. Nelson also adopted the regressive method, and emphasized the role of abstraction in philosophizing. Based on the reception of Fries' views, Nelson formed his own through a critique of contemporaneous Neo-Kantian philosophers. His attack against Neo-Kantianism in his earliest period was based on a defense of Fries' philosophy from its portrayal as psychologism; this led Nelson to criticize Cohen's interpretation of Fries' philosophy. Meanwhile, Nelson's book, *On the So-called Problem of Cognition*, emphasized the impossibility of objective justification of philosophical cognition, and criticized Rickert from this perspective. Nelson's philosophy featured similarities to the analytic tradition, principally in his conception of the Socratic method.

As shown above, Fries' philosophical method significantly influenced the later world of philosophy and science through its revival by the Friesian and Neo-Friesian schools.

Bibliography

Fries, Jakob Friedrich. [1801]: **DPI:** *Dissertatio Philosophica de intuitu intellectuali*, Jena: Typis prageri et soc. (*Philosophical Dissertation on Intellectual Intuition*)
———. [1837–1840]: **GPh, I–II:** *Die Geschichte der Philosophie dargestellt nach den Fortschritten ihrer wissenschaftlichen Entwicklung, Band I–II*, Halle: Verlag der Buchhandlung des Waisenhauses. (*History of Philosophy Described According to Its Scientific Development*)
———. [1807]: **NKV, I–III:** *Neue Kritik der Vernunft, Band I–III*, Heidelberg: Wohr und Zimmer. (*New Critique of Reason*)
———. [1829–1831]: **NaKV, I–III:** *Neue oder anthropologische Kritik der Vernunft, Band I—III, zweite Auflage*, Heidelberg: Christian Friedrich Winter. (*New or Anthropological Critique of Reason*)
———. [1832]: **R:** *Handbuch der Religionsphilosophie und philosophische Aesthetik*, Heidelberg: Christian Friedrich Winter. (*Handbook of Philosophy of Religion and Philosophical Aesthetics*)
———. [1803]: **RFS:** *Reinhold, Fichte und Schelling*, Leibzig: August Lebrecht Reinicke. (*Reinhold, Fichte, and Schelling*)
———. [1819]: **SL:** *System der Logik. Ein Handbuch für Lehrer und zum Selbstgebrauch*, Heidelberg: Wohr und Zimmer. (*System of Logic: A Handbook for Teachers and Self-Use*)
———. [1824]: **SM:** *System der Metaphysik. Ein Handbuch für Lehrer und zum Selbstgebrauch*, Heidelberg: Christian Friedrich Winter. (*System of Metaphysics: A Handbook for Teachers and Self-Use*)
———. [1804]: **SPh:** *System der Philosophie als evidente Wissenschaft*, Leipzig: Johann Conrad Hinrichs. (*System of Philosophy as an Evident Science*)
———. [1798]: **VePM:** "Ueber das Verhältniß der empirischen Psychologie zur Metaphysik", in: *Psychologisches Magazin, Band III*, ed. by Carl Christian Erhard Schmid, Jena: im Cröckerschen Verlag. (*On the Relationship of Empirical Psychology to Metaphysics*)
———. [1805]: **WGA:** *Wissen, Glaube und Ahndung*, Jena: J.C.G. Göpferdt. (*Knowledge, Belief, and Aesthetic Sense*)

Bibliography

Apelt, Ernst Friedrich. [1847]: "Vorrede", in: *Abhandlungn der Fries'schen Schule von Apelt, Schleiden, Schlömilch und Schmid*, Leipzig: Verlag von Wilh. Engelmann, S. 3–6. ("Introduction", in: *Papers of the Friesian School*)

———. [1854]: *Die Theorie der Induction*, Leipzig: Verlag von Wilhelm Engelmann. (*The Theory of Induction*)

———. [1857]: *Metaphysik*, Leipzig: Verlag von Wilhelm Engelmann. (*Metaphysics*)

Schleiden, Matthias Jacob. [1846]: *Grundriss der Botanik zum Gebrauch bei seinen Vorlesungen*, Wihelm Eugelmann: Leipzig. (*Outline of Botany for the Use in Lectures*)

———. [1861]: *Grundzüge der Wissenschaftlichen Botanik nebst einer Methodologischen Einleitung als Anleitung zum Studium der Pflanze*, 4ter Auflage, Wihelm Eugelmann: Leipzig. (*Elements of Scientific Botany with a Methodological Introduction*)

Nelson, Leonard. [1904]: "Die Kritische Methode und das Verhältnis der Psychologie zur Philosophie. Ein Kapitel aus der Methodenlehre", in: *Abhandlungen der Friesschen Schule*. Neue Folge, Vol. 1–1, S. 1–88. (*The Critical Method and the Relationship of Psychology to Philosophy: A Chapter from the Methodology*)

———. [1905]: "Jakob Friedrich Fries und seine jüngsten Kritiker", in: *Abhandlungen der Friesschen Schule*. Neue Folge, Vol. 1–2, S. 233–319. (*Jakob Friedrich Fries and His Recent Critics*)

———. [1908]: *Über das sogenannte Erkenntnisproblem*, Göttingen: Vandenhoeck & Reprecht. (*On the So-called Problem of Cognition*)

———. [1912]: "Die Unmöglichkeit der Erkenntnistheorie: Vortrag gehalten am 11. April 1911 auf dem 4. internationalen Kongress für Philosophie in Bologna", in: *Abhandlungen der Friesschen Schule*. Neue Folge, Vol.3, S. 583–617. (*The Impossibility of Theory of Cognition: A Speech made on 11 April 1911 at the 4th International Congress for Philosophy in Bologna*)

———. [1915]: *Ethische Methodenlehre*, Leipzig: Verlag von Veit und Comp. (*Ethical Methodology*)

———. [1931]: *Die sokratische Methode. Vortrag gehalten am 11. Dezember 1922 in der Pädagogischen Gesellschaft.in Göttingen*, Göttingen: Verlag "Öffentliches Leben". (*The Socratic Method. A Speech made on 11 December 1922 at the Pedagogical Society in Göttingen*)

Kant, Immanuel. [1910ff]: **AA, I–XXIII:** *Kants gesammelte Schriften. Herausgegeben von*. Berlin: Königlich Preussischen Akademie der Wissenschaften.

———. [1998]. **KrV:** *Kritik der reinen Vernunft, Nach der ersten und zweiten Originalausgabe herausgegeben von Jens Timmermann* [1781=A, 1787=B], Hamburg: Felix Meine. (*Critique of Pure Reason*)

Hegel, Georg Wilhelm Friedrich. [1981]. **GW12:** *Georg Wilhelm Friedrich Hegel, Gesammelte Werke, Band 12: Wissenschaft der Logik. Zweiter Band. Die subjektive Logik (1816)*, ed. by Friedrich Hogemann and Walter Jaeschke, Hamburg: Felix Meiner.

———. [2009]. **GW14:** *Gesammelte Werke, Band 14, 1: Grundlinien der Philosophie des Rechts Naturrecht und Staatswissenschaft im Grundrisse – Grundlinien der Philosophie des Rechts*, ed. by Klaus Grotsch and Elisabeth Weisser-Lohmann, Hamburg: Felix Meiner.

Bibliography 99

Beiser, Frederick. [2014]: *The Genesis of Neo-Kantianism, 1796–1880*, Oxford: Oxford University Press.

Blenche, Erna. [1978]: "Zur Geschichte der Neuen Fries'schen Schule und der Jakob Friedrich Fries-Gesellschaft", in: *Archiv für Geschichte der Philosophie*, Vol. 60–2, S. 199–208.

Bonnet, Christian. [2013]: *L'Autre École de Iéna: Critique, métaphysique et psychologie chez Jacob Friedrich Fries*, Paris: Classique Garnier.

Bonsiepen, Wolfgang. [1997]: *Die Begründung einer Naturphilosophie bei Kant, Schelling, Fries und Hegel: Mathematische versus spekulative Naturphilosophie, Philosophische Abhandlungen, Bd. 70*, Frankfurt am Main: Vittorio Klostermann.

———. [2004]: "*Philosophie, Nichtphilosophie und Unphilosophie*", in: *Friedrich Heinrich Jacobi: Ein Wendepunkt der geistigen Bildung der Zeit*, ed. by Walter Jaeschke and Birgit Sandkaulen, Hamburg: Felix Meiner Verlag, S. 257–277.

Cassirer, Ernst. [1920]: *Das Erkenntnisproblem in der Philosophie und Wissenschaft der neueren Zeit. Dritter Band, Die nachkantische Systeme*, Berlin: Verlag Bruno Cassirer.

———. [1950]: *The Problem of Knowledge: Philosophy, Science and History since Hegel*, translated by William H. Woglom and Charls W. Hendel, London: Yale University Press.

Conant, James [2019]: "Some Socratic Aspects of Wittgenstein's Conception of Philosophy", in: *Wittgenstein on Philosophy, Objectivity, and Meaning*, ed. by James Conant and Sebastian Sunday, Cambridge University Press, S. 231–264.

Cohen, Hermann. [1871]: *Kants Theorie der Erfahrung*, Berlin: Harrwitz und Gossmann.

———. [1885]: *Kants Theorie der Erfahrung, zweite neubearbeitete Auflage*, Berlin: Harrwitz und Gossmann.

Eggeling, Heinrich. [1875]: "Apelt, Ernst Friedrich", in: *Allgemeine Deutsche Biographie*, Band I, S. 502–504.

Erdmann, Johann Eduard. [1866]: *Grundriss der Geschichte der Philosophie, Zweiter und letzter Band: Philosophie der Neuzeit*, Berlin: Verlag von Wilhelm Hertz.

Fichte, Johann Gottlieb. [1970]: *Gesamtausgabe der Bayerischen Akademie der Wissenschaften, Band I,4: Werke 1797–1798*, ed. by R. Lauth, H. Jacob and H. Gliwitzky, Stuttfart-Bad Cannstatt.

Fischer, Kuno. [1862]: *Die beiden kantischen Schulen in Jena: Rede zum Antritt des Prorektorats, den 1 Februar 1862*, Stuttgart: Gotta'scher Verlag.

———. [1898]: *Geschichte der neuern Philosophie, Jubiläumsausgabe, neunter Band. Schopenhauers Leben, Werke und Lehre, zweite und bearbeitete und vermehrte Auflage*, Heidelberg: Carl Winter's Universitätsbuchhandlung.

———. [1901]: *Geschichte der neuern Philosophie, Jubiläumsausgabe, Achter Band. Hegels Leben, Werke und Lehre, II Theil*. Heidelberg: Carl Winter's Universitätsbuchhandlung.

Franke, Holger. [1991]: *Leonard Nelson Ein biographischer Beitrag unter besonderer Berücksichtigung seiner rechts- und staatsphilosophischen Arbeiten*, Ammersbek: Verlag an der Lottbek P. Jensen.

Fujita, Masakatsu. [2004]: "Remarks", in: *Nishida Kitaro: Complete Works*, Vol. 15, Tokyo: Iwanami Shoten.

100 Bibliography

Fukutani, Shigeru [2009]: *Saggi sulla filosofia kantiana*, Chisen Shokan (in Japanese).

Glock, Hans-Johann. [2011]: "Nelson und die analytische Philosophie", in: *Leonard Nelson — ein früher Denker der analytischen Philosophie? Ein Symposium zum 80 Todestag des Göttinger Philosophen*, ed. by Armin A. Berger, J. Schroth, and G. Raupach-Strey, Lit-Verlag, pp. 39–70.

Grundl, Wolfgang Josef [2006]: *Die Psychische Anthropologie von Jakob Friedrich Fries – eine historisch-systematische Diskussion zur Philosophie des Geistes*. Inaugural-Dissertation zur Erlangung des Doktorgrades der Philosophie an der Julius-Maximilians-Universität zu Würzburg vorgelegt von Wolfgang Josef Grundl aus München.

Habermas, Jürgen. [2019]: *Auch eine Geschichte der Philosophie, 2 Bände*, Berlin: Suhrkamp.

Hasselblatt, Meinhard. [1922]: *Jacob Friedrich Fries: Seine Philosophie und seine Persönlichkeit, Eine einführenden Darstellung*, München: Rösl & Cie.

Hatfield, Gary. [1990]: *The Natural and the Normative: Theories of Spatial Perception from Kant to Helmholtz*, Cambridge, MA and London: MIT Press.

Hayakawa, Jiro. [1986]: "Fries und Psychologismus (1)", in: *The Waseda Journal of General Science*, Vol. 30, pp. 1–20 (written in Japanese).

———. [1987a]: "Fries und Psychologismus (2)", in: *The Waseda Journal of General Science*, Vol. 31, pp. 89–105 (written in Japanese).

———. [1987b]: "Fries und Psychologismus (3)", in: *The Waseda Journal of General Science*, Vol. 32, pp. 145–159 (written in Japanese).

Heidegger, Martin. [1987]: "Zur Bestimmung der Philosophie", in: *Martin Heidegger: Gesamtausgabe, II. Abteilung: Vorlesung, Band 56/57*, Frankfurt am Main: Vittorio Klostermann.

Herbart, Johann Friedrich. [1808]: "Hauptpunkte der Metaphysik", in: *J.F. Herbart's kleinere philosophische Schriften und Abhandlungen, nebst dessen wissenschaftlichem Nachlasse, Erster Band*, ed. by Gustav Hartenstein, Leipzig: F.A. Brockhaus, 1842.

Herbart, Johann Friedrich. [1828]: *Allgemeine Metaphysik nebst den Anfängen der philosophischen Naturlehre, Erster, historisch-kritischer Teil*, Königsberg: August Wilhelm Unzer.

Hermut Pulte. [2006]: "Kant, Fries, and the Expanding Universe of Science", in: *The Kantian Legacy in Nineteenth-Century Science*, ed. by Michael Friedman and Alfred Nordmann, London: The MIT Press, pp. 101–122.

———. [2013]: "J.F. Fries' Philosophy of Science, the New Friesian School and the Berlin Group: On Divergent Scientific Philosophies, Difficult Relations and Missed Opportunities", in: *The Berlin Group and the Philosophy of Logical Empiricism*, ed. by Nikolay Milkov and Volker Peckhaus, Dordrecht/Heidelberg/New York/London: Springer, pp. 43–66.

Herrmann, Kay. [2000]: *Mathematische Naturphilosophie in der Grundlagendiskussion: Jakob Friedrich Fries und die Wissenschaft*, Göttingen: Vandenhoeck & Ruprecht.

———. [2011]: "Leonard Nelson und die Naturwissenschaften", in: *Leonard Nelson — ein früher Denker der analytischen Philosophie? Ein Symposium zum*

80 Todestag des Göttinger Philosophen, ed. by Armin A. Berger, J. Schroth, and G. Raupach-Strey, Berlin: Lit-Verlag, pp. 169–191.

Hirschberger, Johannes. [1961]: *Kleine Philosophiegeschichte*, Freiburg: Verlag Herder.

Jacobi, Friedrich Heinrich. [1811]: *Von den Göttlichen Dingen und ihrer Offenbarung*, Leipzig: Gerhard Fleischer dem Jüngern.

Jahn, I. [1991]: "The Influence of Jakob Friedrich Fries on Matthias Schleiden", in: *World Views and Scientific Discipline Formation: Boston Studies in the Philosophy of Science*, Vol. 134, ed. by W.R. Woodward and R.S. Cohen, Dordrecht: Springer.

Janssen, Paul. [1989]: "Psychologismus", in: *Historisches Wörterbuch der Philosophie, Band 7: P–Q*, ed. by Joachim Ritter and Karlfried Gründer, Basel: Schwabe & Co. AG Verlag, pp. 1675–1678.

Kastil, Alfred. [1912]: *Jacob Friedrich Fries' Lehre von der unmittelbaren Erkenntnis*, Göttingen: Vandenhoeck & Ruprecht.

Kinkel, Walter. [1903]: *Joh. Fr. Herbart: Sein Leben und seine Philosophie*, Giessen: J. Ricker'sche Verlagsbuchhandlung.

Liebmann, Otto. [1865]: *Kant und die Epigonen: Eine kritische Abhandlung*, Stuttgart: Karl Schoder.

Leary, D.E. [1982]: "The Psychology of Jakob Friedrich Fries (1773–1843): Its Context, Nature, and historical Significance", in: *Storia E Critica Della Psicologia*, Vol. 3, No.2, pp. 217–248.

Milkov, Nikolay. [2012]: "Karl Popper's Debt to Leonard Nelson", in: *Grazer Philosophische Stidien*, Vol. 86, pp. 137–156.

Nishida, Kitaro. [2004a]: "Introduction to Philosophy", in: *Nishida Kitaro: Complete Works*, Vol. 15, Tokyo: Iwanami Shoten, pp. 153–315.

———. [2004b]: "Study of Religion", in: *Nishida Kitaro: Complete Works*, Vol. 15, Tokyo: Iwanami Shoten, pp. 3–152.

Oota, Tadahiro. [2019]: "Jakob Friedrich Fries as an opponent of German Idealism", in: *Anti/Idealism: Re-interpreting a German Discourse*, ed. by Gert Hofmann and Juliana Albuquerque, München: De Gruyter, pp. 87–102.

Platner, Ernst. [1795]: *Lehrbuch der Logik und Metaphysik*, Leipzig: Schwickertschen Verlag.

Popper, Karl. [1935]: *Logik der Forschung. Zur Erkenntnistheorie der modernen Naturwissenschaft*, Vienna: Springer-Verlag.

———. [1959]: *The Logic of Scientific Discovery*, London and New York: Hutchinson & Co.

———. [1979]: *Die beiden Grundprobleme der Erkenntnistheorie: Aufgrund von Manuskripten aus den Jahren 1930–1933*, ed. by Troels Eggers Hansen, Tübingen: J.C.B. Mohr. (English translation: *The Two Fundamental Problems of the Theory of Knowledge*, translated by Andreas Pickel, ed. by Troels Eggers Hansen, London and New York: Routledge, 2009).

Redaelli, Roberto. [2016]: *Per una logica dell'umano. Antropologia filosofica e Wertlehre in Windelband, Rickert e Lask* (dissertation, Università degli Studi di Milano)

Rickert, Heinrich. [1904]: *Der Gegenstand der Erkenntnis: Einführung in die Transzendentalphilosophie*, zweite, verbesserte und erweiterte Auflage, Tübingen and Leipzig: J.C.B. Mohr.

Röd, Wolfgang. [1996]: *Der Weg der Philosophie von den Anfängen bis ins 20. Jahrhundert. Zweiter Band: 17. bis 20. Jahrhundert*, München: Verlag C.H. Beck.

Roberto, Davide. [2007]: *Kant e Fries: Significato e legittimità della "svolta anthropologica"*, Milano: Edizioni Unicopli.

Schopenhauer, Arthur. [1967]: *Der Handschriftliche Nachlaß, Band 2, Herausgegeben von Arthur Hübscher*, Frankfurt: Waldemar Kramer.

Tennemann, Wilhelm Gottlieb. [1798ff.]: *Geschichte der Philosophie, 12 Bände*, Leipzig: Johann Ambrosius Barth.

Vogel, Emil Ferdinand. [1843]: *Schelling oder Hegel oder Keiner von Beyden?: Ein Separat-Dotum über die Eigenthümlichkeiten der neueren deutschen Philosophie, mit besonderer Beziehung auf die, von Herrn GH. Prof. D. Friedrich Jacob Fries zu Jena in seiner „Geschichte der Philosophie" neuerlich hierüber ausgesprochen Ansichten*, Leipzig: Verlag der Rein'schen Buchhandlung.

Whitehead, Alfred North. [1929]: *Process and Reality: An Essay in Cosmology*, New York: Free Press.

Windelband, Wilhelm. [1880]: *Die Geschichte der neuern Philosophie in ihrem Zusammenhange mit der allgemeinen Curtur und den besonderen Wissenschaften, Zweiter Band: Von Kant bis Hegel und Herbart*, Leipzig: Breitkopf & Härtel.

Zeltner, Hermann. [1953]: "Apelt, Ernst Friedrich", in: *Neue Deutsche Biographie*, Band I, S. 323–324.

Index

Note: Page numbers followed by "n" refer to notes.

absolute intuition 39
abstraction 18–20, 22, 30, 40, 58, 59; critique based on 38–39; induction vs. 61–62, 68–70, 87–88; philosophical 61; qualitative 37, 38, 94; quantitative 37–38, 94
actuality 54, 64–66, 73
aesthetic feeling 44
aesthetic sense (*Ahndung*) 13, 41, 44
affection 32
analogy/analogous 36, 40, 45, 46, 69, 95
analytic 12, 34–38, 40, 43, 52, 65, 82–85, 88, 89, 94, 96; abstraction *see* qualitative abstraction; method 19
anthropology 7–9, 11, 93; philosophical 34
anti-Semitism 14n3
Apelt, Ernst Friedrich 4, 58, 77, 78, 90n34; Friesian School *see* Friesian School; *Metaphysics* 58–59, 64–66, 96; *Papers of the Friesian School* (*Abhandlungen der Fries'schen Schule*) 59; and Schleiden, relationship between 67–68; *Theory of Induction* (*Die Theorie der Induction*), *The* 58, 60–63, 95
Apelt, Otto 90n39
apodictic/apodictically 17, 24, 27, 28, 34, 35, 39, 42, 43, 52, 53, 57, 78
apodicticity 17, 24, 27, 28, 34–35, 43, 52, 53n62, 78

appearance 41, 47–50, 81, 95
apperception 30, 63, 78, 79
apriority 28, 53n62
arbitrary 4, 29, 30, 32, 33, 35, 65
Aristotelian 38, 87
Aristotelian abstraction *see* qualitative abstraction
Aristotle 87, 88
arithmetic 88
astronomy 59
Attempt at a New Presentation of the Science of Knowledge, An (Fries) 37
Auch eine Geschichte der Philosophie (Habermas) 4
beauty 19, 41–44, 46, 95
being 20, 21, 26, 31, 36, 41–43, 47, 48, 50, 59, 67, 81, 83, 87, 92, 95

Beiser, Frederick 48, 52n36, 54n80, 55n89; *Genesis of Neo-Kantianism: 1796–1880, The* 5
belief (*Glaube*) 13, 17, 40, 41, 44–47, 49, 50, 54, 95
Beneke, Friedrich Eduard 5, 9
Berg, Otto 90n39
Berger, Armin 92n70
Bernays, Paul 96
Bonsiepen, Wolfgang 54n74, 55n98
botany 58, 67, 96
Bousset, Wilhelm 13
Brinkmann, Carl 90n41
Brucker, Johann Jakob 3

Cassirer, Ernst 20, 68, 90n31; Fries' philosophy through Apelt's *Metaphysics*, interpretation of 66
categories 23, 29–31, 44, 53n50, 54n68, 55n98
causality 2, 17, 20, 40, 45, 95
cell theory 69–70
cognition 20; human 17, 25, 29, 48–50, 56n104, 67; immediate 18, 21–24, 29–31, 33–35, 48, 52n36, 54nn68, 72, 84, 55n89, 58–60, 62–66, 69, 71, 74–76, 84, 94, 96; mathematical 66; metaphysical 53n56, 65, 66; modes of 13, 44; philosophical *see* philosophical cognition; *a posteriori* 7–8, 25, 26, 39, 94; *a priori* 7–8, 24–27, 34, 35, 39, 42–43, 53n50, 55–56n104, 57n132, 64, 66, 94; self-cognition 11, 25, 26, 31, 51n18; synthetic 54n79; transcendental 24, 25, 94
Cohen, Hermann: critique, Nelson's stance against 77–79; *Kant's Theory of Experience* 77
consciousness 20, 25, 39, 51–52n18; theory of 56n106
consensus (*verständigen*) 17
"consensus-building" (*Verständigung*) 85
construction 40, 64
conviction (*Überzeugung*) 13
critical 2, 4, 6, 17, 22, 26, 44, 51, 59, 63, 67, 69, 73, 76, 77
Critique of Practical Reason (Kant) 19
critique of reason, Fries' conception of: anthropological investigation 24–26; apodicticity of philosophical cognition 24; conventional evaluation 26; deduction 22–24; empiricist standpoint 28; memorized line of thought *vs.* logical line of thought 32–33; method of philosophy, formation of 35–40; methodological standpoint in philosophy 16–35; Nelson's response 27; philosophizing, method of 16–18, 28; psychology, role of 33–34; regressive method, adopting 18–20; speculation 22, 29, 33, 52nn31, 34; theory of reason, need for 20–22

deduction (*Deduktion*) 21–24, 27, 30, 34, 40, 46, 47, 52n36, 55n89, 62, 69, 74–76, 78, 91n51, 94; transcendental 84
descriptive 72
dogmatic 44, 63, 64, 68, 73
dogmatism 28, 36, 43, 54n72, 68, 78

Elements of Scientific Botany (*Grundzüge der Wissenschaftlichen Botanik*) (Schleiden) 58
Elsenhans, Theodor 72
empirical 6–10, 12, 13, 16, 23, 26, 27, 32, 34–36, 42, 43, 45, 47, 48, 63, 65, 67, 68, 94; psychology 6, 8; science 25
empiricism 28, 34, 36, 54, 61, 63, 78
Erdmann, Johann Eduard 93; *Outline of the History of Philosophy* (*Grundrisss der Geschichte der Philosophie*) 8
essence 6, 7, 18, 27, 41–43, 50, 61, 74, 95
eternal truth 48
ethical 17, 41–46, 86–88, 95
ethics 45–47, 86–88, 92n83
exhibition (*Aufweisung*) 23, 29, 52, 74, 84, 88, 89n15, 94
experience 9, 20, 24–26, 28, 30, 33, 34, 36, 37, 43–45, 49, 52n34, 53n62, 55n102, 56nn104–105, 58, 61, 63, 70, 71, 73, 76, 77, 94

feeling of truth (*Wahrheitsgefühl*) 40–47, 56nn128–129, 131, 57n137, 94, 95; centralization of 45–46; descriptions of 41–42; role of 42–46
Fichte, Johann Gottlieb 1–5, 7, 14n16, 16, 28, 35–40, 42, 43, 47, 53nn51–52, 57n137, 59, 72, 82, 94
finitude 17, 44, 48–50, 56
Fischer, Kuno 2, 25, 26, 53n50, 72; critique of Fries' philosophy 7–8
form of judgment 31, 54n84, 65
form of thinking 33
form of understanding 31
Francke, Holger 91n56
freedom 2, 21, 23
Fries, Jakob Friedrich 1, 4–6; *Attempt at a New Presentation of the Science*

of Knowledge, An 37; critique of reason, conception of 16–40; *Grounding of Science of Knowledge* 37; *Handbook of Philosophy of Religion* 41, 46; *Handbook of Psychic Anthropology* 9; *Knowledge, Belief, and Aesthetic Sense* 13, 40–41, 45, 47–50; *New Critique of Reason* (*Neue Kritik der Vernunft*) 6, 7, 9, 11, 16, 25, 28, 34–40, 42, 45, 47, 56–57n131, 94, 95; "On the Relationship of Empirical Psychology to Metaphysics" 35; *Outlines of the Philosophy of Right* (*Grundlinien der Philosophie des Rechts*) 11; Reinhold, Fichte, and Schelling 38, 42–44, 47; "Speech on the German Student Union" (*Rede an die deutschen Burschen*) 11; *System of Logics* (*System der Logik*) 11, 12, 29, 89n15; *System of Metaphysics* 41, 45–46, 64

Friesian School (*Fries'sche Schule*) 40; Apelt's views of 60–66; philosophical development of 58–71; rise of 59–60

Fries' philosophy in history of philosophy 6–10; contemporary schematization 10–11; Hegelian philosophers' critique 7–8; Hegel's reading of 11–12; Herbart's assessment 6–7; Neo-Kantian philosophers' schematization 8–10; Nishida's understanding of 12–13; problem with reception of 10–13

Fukutani, Shigeru 2

General Metaphysics and the Beginnings of the Philosophical Doctrine of Nature (*Allgemeine Metaphysik, nebst den Anfängen der philosophischen Naturlehre*) (Herbart) 6–7
general presupposition 17, 19, 21, 24, 32, 34, 37, 54, 85, 86
general principle 20, 22, 24, 61, 62, 70, 76
general proposition 20, 61, 62, 70, 76
Genesis of Neo-Kantianism: 1796–1880, The (Beiser) 5

geometry 64
German idealism 1, 3–7, 13, 16, 35, 50, 58, 82, 90, 93, 95
Geschichte der Philosophie (Tennemann) 3
Glock, Hans-Johann 85, 92n77
God 21
Goesch, Heinrich 90n41
good 19, 44, 46
Grelling, Kurt 83, 84, 96
grounding (*Grundlegung*) 19, 20, 27, 54n72
Grounding for the Metaphysics of Morals (Kant) 19
Grounding of Science of Knowledge (Fries) 37
Grundl, Wolfgang Josef 11, 19

Habermas, Jürgen: *Auch eine Geschichte der Philosophie* 4
Handbook of Philosophy of Religion (Fries) 41, 46
Handbook of Psychic Anthropology (Fries) 9
Hasselblatt, Meinhard 54n84
Hatfield, Gary 10, 52n34
Hegel, Wilhelm Friedrich 1–5, 7; "Note on Fries" (*Notiz zu Fries*) 11, 12; reading of Fries' philosophy 11–12
Hegelianism 5, 83, 93
Hegelian philosophers' critique 7–8
Heidegger, Martin 92n69
Herbart, Johann Friedrich 5; *General Metaphysics and the Beginnings of the Philosophical Doctrine of Nature* (*Allgemeine Metaphysik, nebst den Anfängen der philosophischen Naturlehre*) 6–7
Hermann, Kay 89n2, 90n39
Hessenberg, Gerhard 90nn38–39
heuristic method 69
Hilbert, David 96
Hirschberger, Johannes 3
history: developmental 68
History of Modern Philosophy (*Geschichte der neueren Philosophie*) (Windelband) 9
history of philosophy 3–5, 26, 87, 90n31, 93; definition of 1–2; Fries' philosophy in 6–13

Index

Hitler, Adolf 14n3
Hölderlin, Johann Christian Friedrich 4
human cognition 17, 25, 29, 48–50, 56n104, 67
Husserl, Edmund 80

idea (*Meinungen*) 17
imagination 32
immediate cognition of reason 18, 21–24, 29–31, 33–35, 48, 52n36, 54nn68, 72, 84, 58–60, 62–66, 69, 71, 74–76, 84, 94, 96; in Apelt's *Metaphysics* 64–66
indifference (*Indifferenz*) 49
induction (*Induktion*) 58–63; abstraction *vs.* 61–62, 68–70, 87–88
inference 22, 32, 65, 76, 87
ingenious 51n4
inner perception 55n103
intellectual 1, 3
intellectual intuition 18, 36–37, 40, 48–50, 94, 95
intuition 19, 21, 23, 24, 28, 30–32, 51n15, 64–66, 75; absolute 39; intellectual 18, 36–37, 40, 48–50, 94, 95

Jacobi, Friedrich Heinrich 4
Jahn, Ilse 90n35
Jakob Friedrich Fries Association (*Jakob Friedrich Fries-Gesellschaft*) 71
judgment (*Urteile*) 54n84, 55n98, 72; form of 31, 54n84, 65
justification (*Begründung*) 21, 23, 58, 74, 75, 80, 81, 84; empirical-psychological 9; of philosophical cognition 22–24, 40, 64, 76, 86

Kaiser, Karl 90n38
Kant, Immanuel 1, 4, 5, 9, 10, 25, 93, 94; on conviction (*Überzeugung*) 13; critical philosophy 2, 16; *Critique of Practical Reason* 19; critique to empirical psychology 7; *Grounding for the Metaphysics of Morals* 19; on philosophizing 17–18; *Prolegomena* 19
Kant's Theory of Experience (Cohen) 77
Kierkegaard, Søren 2

knowledge (*Wissen*) 13, 41, 44; immediate 63
Knowledge, Belief, and Aesthetic Sense (Fries) 13, 40–41, 45, 47–50
Kohsaka, Masaaki 13
Kraft, Julius 84

language 7, 9, 85
Leibniz, Gottfried Wilhelm 60, 61
Liebmann, Otto 8–9, 26, 48, 51, 77, 93; critique of Fries' philosophy 9
life 17–19, 22, 28, 34, 37, 41, 46, 61, 64, 68, 69, 71, 72, 87, 94
logical 32–33
Logic of Scientific Discovery, The (Popper) 63
Logik der Forschung (Popper) 63
Lotze, Hermann 59

material 12, 70
mathematical cognition 66
mathematics 20, 22, 23, 45, 59, 64, 71, 74, 90n34, 95
maxim 89n15
mediated (*mittelbar*) 31
memory 32–33
metaphysical cognition 66; homogeneity (*Gleichartigkeit*) of 65
metaphysics: critique *vs.* 27; object of critique 35–36; system, construction of 40–51
Metaphysics (Apelt) 58–59, 64–66, 96; immediate cognition of reason in 64–66
method of philosophy 51n1; formation of 35–40; intellectual intuition 36–37; metaphysical system, construction of 40–51; object of critique, in *New Critique of Reason* 38–39; sophistication of, in *New Critique of Reason* 37–38; views on psychology and metaphysics 35–36
Meyer, Bona 77
Meyerhof, Otto 90n39
Milkov, Nicolay 84
mind 32, 48, 56n105
Mirbt, Ernst Sigismund 89n2
morality 45

Natorp, Paul 80
natural philosophy 40, 59, 67, 68, 87
natural science 40, 44, 58–60, 66–69, 71, 73, 86
nature (*Inbegriff*) 27
Nelson, Leonard 4, 5, 13, 14n3, 25, 34, 54n79; critique of Rickert's views 79–82; Fries' philosophy, reception of 72–76; Neo-Friesian school *see* Neo-Friesian school (*Neufries'sche Schule*); *Papers of Fries' School: New Series* (*Abhandlungen der Fries'schen Schule: Neue Folge*) 71; response to critique of reason 27; *On the So-called Problem of Cognition* 96; stance against Cohen's critique 77–79
Neo-Friesian school (*Neufries'sche Schule*) 4, 40; and analytic tradition 82–89; battle against Neo-Kantianism 76–82; historical relationship to analytic philosophy 83–84; linguistic analysis 85–86; rise of 71; socratic method 86–88
Neo-Kantianism 5, 93; Neo-Friesian school's battle against 76–82
Neo-Kantian movement 4, 71, 76, 91n55
New Critique of Reason (*Neue Kritik der Vernunft*) (Fries) 6, 7, 9, 11, 16, 25, 28, 34–40, 42, 45, 47, 56–57n131, 94, 95; feeling of truth (*Wahrheitsgefühl*) *see* feeling of truth (*Wahrheitsgefühl*); method of philosophy, sophistication of 37–38; object of critique in 38–39
Niethammer, Friedrich Phillip Immanuel 4
Nietzsche, Friedrich 2
nineteenth-century German philosophy 2–3; dominant schematization of 3–4; problem of 4–6
Nishida, Kitaro 3; Fries' philosophy, understanding of 12–13; "Introduction to Philosophy" 13; "Philosophy and Religion" 13; "Study of Religion" 13
"Note on Fries" (*Notiz zu Fries*) (Hegel) 11, 12

objects of philosophy, extension of 44–46
"On the Relationship of Empirical Psychology to Metaphysics" (Fries) 35
On the So-called Problem of Cognition (Nelson) 96
opinions (*Beurteilunngen*) 18–19, 28, 29, 34, 41, 42, 54nn72, 80, 72, 85, 89n15
organic 70
organism 67, 68, 70
Otto, Rudolf 13
Outline of the History of Philosophy (*Grundrisss der Geschichte der Philosophie*) (Erdmann) 8
Outlines of the Philosophy of Right (*Grundlinien der Philosophie des Rechts*) (Fries) 11

Papers of the Friesian School (*Abhandlungen der Fries'schen Schule*) (Apelt) 59
perception 19–21, 24, 25, 30, 32–34, 36, 43, 45, 53n62, 55n103; inner 55n103
phenomenology 80, 84, 85
philosophical anthropology 34
philosophical cognition 17, 19, 20–23, 25, 29–31, 33–37, 39–47, 51n18, 53n57, 54n73, 57n133, 59, 64–66, 71, 72, 82, 84–86, 94, 96; apodicticity of 24, 28; apriority of 28, 53n62; development of 42–46; investigation of 22; justification of 22–24, 40, 64, 76, 86; problem of justifying 72–76; *see also* cognition
philosophizing (*Kunst zu philosophieren*): art of 22, 24, 29, 33; method of 16–18, 28, 85–86; psychology for 34
philosophy: history 1–13, 26, 87, 90n31, 93; method of 35–51; natural 40, 59, 67, 68, 87; objects of 44–46; as a science 18, 25, 33
physics 52n34, 67; metaphysics *see* metaphysics
Platonic abstraction *see* qualitative abstraction
Plattner, Ernst 55n94

Popper, Karl 84; Fries' philosophy in his *Theory of Induction*, reception of 62–63; *Logic of Scientific Discovery, The* 63; *Logik der Forschung* 63; *Two Fundamental Problems of the Theory of Knowledge, The* 63
progressive 36, 72–74, 82, 87, 94
Prolegomena (Kant) 19
psychologism 7–10, 33–34, 93
psychology 9, 11, 56n105, 72; empirical 6, 8; object of critique 35–36
Pulte, Hermut 90n34
purpose 2, 18, 21, 24, 28, 40

qualitative abstraction 37, 38, 94
quantitative abstraction 37–38, 94

rationalistic speculation 61
reality 44, 47, 64, 65
reason (*Vernunft*): critique of 16–40; immediate cognition of 18, 21–24, 29–31, 33–35, 48, 52n36, 54nn68, 72, 84, 55n89, 58–60, 62–66, 69, 71, 74–76, 84, 94, 96; self-confidence of 46, 75, 76; and understanding (*Verstand*), distinction between 28–31
receptivity 29
recognition 28
"re-consciousness" (*Wiederbewusstsein*) 20, 33, 39, 51n18, 66, 90n31
Redaelli, Roberto 92n69
regression 20, 61, 87
regressive method 38; adopting 18–20
Reinhold, Fichte, and Schelling (Fries) 38, 42–44, 47
Reinhold, Karl Leonhard 4, 7, 17–19, 28, 36, 47, 53n51, 72, 82
religion 13, 17, 46
representation 20, 22, 25, 28, 29, 31–33, 37, 38, 47, 48, 55n103, 65
Rickert, Heinrich 80–82, 91n66
Röd, Wolfgang 66, 76
Rüstow, Alexander 90n41

Scheler, Max 72
Schelling, Friedrich Wilhelm Joseph von 1–5, 7, 25, 35–40

schematization 3–4; contemporary, of Fries' philosophy 10–11; Neo-Kantian philosophers' 8–10
scheme 5, 37, 84
Schleiden, Matthias Jacob 59; and Apelt, relationship between 67–68; *Elements of Scientific Botany* (*Grundzüge der Wissenschaftlichen Botanik*) 58; emphasis on Fries' philosophy 62–63; induction and abstraction, distinction between 68–70; methodological perspective 66–70
Schleiermacher, Friedrich Daniel Ernst 13
Schlömilch, Oskar Xavier 89n2
Schopenhauer, Arthur 11
science of knowledge 36, 37
scientific system theory 62
self-activity (*Selbsttätigkeit*) 29
self-cognition 11, 25, 26, 31, 51n18
self-consciousness 31
self-observation (*Selbstbeobachtung*) 25, 26, 31, 69, 72, 73, 82
sensationality (*Empfänglichkeit*) 29
sensibility 31, 32, 51n15, 54n72
sign 68
society 2
Socrates 86–88, 92n81
socratic method 86–88
soul 46, 68
space 31, 38, 50, 53n50, 64, 65
speculation 22, 29, 33, 52nn31, 34; rationalistic 61
spirit 3, 9, 17, 20–22, 25, 26, 31, 36, 53n50, 55n102, 59, 60, 70
spontaneity 29
subject 1, 26, 48, 70, 74, 75, 80, 81, 84, 91n51
sublimity 41, 95
substance 21, 40, 95
synthetic abstraction *see* quantitative abstraction
synthetic cognition 54n79
system: metaphysics, construction of 40–51
System of Logics (*System der Logik*) (Fries) 11, 12, 29, 89n15
System of Metaphysics (Fries) 41, 45–46, 64

Tennemann, Wilhelm Gottlieb: *Geschichte der Philosophie* 3
Thales 1
theory of cognition: impossibility of 79–80
Theory of Induction (*Die Theorie der Induction*), *The* (Apelt) 58, 60–63, 95
theory of reason, need for 20–22
thing in itself: as aspect of things 49–50; in Fries' philosophy 47–50; and transcendental truth 49; truth and exclusion of 48–49
thinking, form of 33
Tractatus (Wittgenstein) 85
transcendental cognition 24, 25, 94
transcendental deduction 84
transcendental philosophy 72, 77
transcendental truth 41, 48, 49; thing in itself and 49
truth 19, 21, 25, 30, 48–49, 75, 76, 81; empirical 48; eternal 48; feeling of (*Wahrheitsgefühl*) 40–47, 56nn128–129, 131, 57n137, 94, 95; geometrical 65; metaphysical 65; necessary 61, 65, 73; philosophical 54n73; theory of 48–50; transcendental 41, 48, 49
Two Fundamental Problems of the Theory of Knowledge, The (Popper) 63

understanding (*Verstand*) 28–35, 43, 54nn80, 84, 62, 65; and reason (*Vernunft*), distinction between 28–31

validity 4, 20, 23, 24, 27, 42, 45, 49, 53n50, 58, 62, 65, 66, 70, 75, 76, 80, 88, 91n66, 94
verification (*Beweis*) 23, 27, 69
virtue 21, 38

Whitehead, Alfred North 1, 14n1
whole 37
will 21, 31, 46, 81, 91n66
Windelband, Wilhelm 26, 53n54, 82, 93; *History of Modern Philosophy* (*Geschichte der neueren Philosophie*) 9
Wittgenstein, Ludwig: *Tractatus* 85
world 31, 46, 76, 96